# Laughing at Life's Lunacies

# Laughing at Life's Lunacies

Amy Faye Sloter

Book Design & Production:
Columbus Publishing Lab
www.ColumbusPublishingLab.com

Cover design by Amy Faye Sloter

Copyright © 2023 by
Amy Faye Sloter
LCCN: 2022907833

Paperback ISBN: 978-1-63337-622-9
E-book ISBN: 978-1-63337-623-6

Printed in the United States of America
1 3 5 7 9 10 8 6 4 2

For Dan Steinman and Ned Siegel, who,
back in 1969 and 1970, during my senior year
at Lakewood High School in Hebron, Ohio, transformed
our English Literature class into a very fond memory.

# Table of Contents

# Introduction

**I was only 17 years old** the first time I ever bellowed with laughter at the lunacies of living. I had just spent the previous two years being told by a dozen different "loving relatives" to get out and never come back because I was no sister (or daughter) of theirs. The final time this occurred, just a month shy of my eighteenth birthday, my younger sister said that if I had to leave, she was coming with me. I tried to make her stay, as I had nowhere to go and no idea where I might go, but she insisted.

So, we were standing in the room we shared, our suitcases spread out on the bed while we solemnly filled them with our few belongings, when Jean thoughtfully observed: "You know, Amy, if we would just keep these packed, it wouldn't take us so long to leave every time someone throws you out."

I started laughing. Then she started laughing, and for at least 10 minutes we laughed and could not stop. The ludicrous insanity of my situation—the sheer stupidity of the two years of the nightmare my relatives were putting me through—had defeated my ability to do anything except laugh at it.

I have been laughing at life's lunacies ever since.

The anecdotes in this book recount some of the many situations I've encountered that got me laughing. Some were crazy, some were so stupid they were almost unbelievable, some were poignant, some were zany, some were just amusingly or gently silly, but all of them were worth laughing at.

# Chapter 1

# Dan and Ned and English Literature

This book came about when Ned Siegel, who, in 1970, graduated with me from Lakewood High School in Hebron, Ohio, sent me a questionnaire pertaining to our 50th senior class reunion. One of the questions was, "What is your favorite Lakewood High School memory?" I filled out Ned's questionnaire and sent it back to him with the following answer:

I have only a few memories because I was there for only those nine months of my senior year, and I was not involved in any activities, nor did I even know any of my classmates. I was just gritting my teeth until I graduated, turned 18, could get away from my family, and leave the first 18 years of my life as far behind me as I could put them. I had been counting off the years since I could count, because I had perceived, even as a toddler, that 18 was the magic age that would set me free. I had seen my older brothers and sisters leave home at that age, so I had put those two facts together real early in life.

Consequently, while at Lakewood, I ignored everything and everyone, both in and out of school, as much as I could. It was only after I had graduated and had the yearbook that I was able to link names with the few faces I had ever genuinely noticed. I was in survival mode back then, for myself and my younger sister, and I just blanked out everyone and everything that wasn't standing in my way. I never suspected I would ever see any of my classmates again.

Among the few distinct memories I have of being at Lakewood, however, Dan Steinman and Ned Siegel in my English Literature class will have to qualify as the "favorite" memory for one simple reason. The rest of my life was so bad during that year that the only joyous thing in it was going in there every day and having Dan make me laugh while I kept up a running friendly argument with Ned that Elvis, not the Beatles, was and would always be the King of Rock and Roll. I took advantage of the one happy component of my existence to have some fun by razzing and twitting Ned about the Beatles and Elvis, although I actually had many favorite singers beyond Elvis. (Roy Orbison had been a favorite since I was 12, Vikki Carr since I was 13, and the first LP I ever bought at age 16 was by Waylon Jennings.)

I remember some girl passing me in the hallway as we neared graduation and telling me that I had been voted "most reserved," and it kind of threw me, because I knew I was not actually "reserved" and the title should have been given to whoever else was in the running. (If I got voted anything nowadays it would be Miss Lives Inside Her Head, because I spend all my time there, clearing out my ceaseless stream of thought by writing it down.)

What surprised me at the time, however, was when Ned said the same thing: that I was not truly reserved. He didn't know the truth—that I had been born old, and I had never been in a position to "be a teenager"—but he was right, and he had realized the truth because he was the one person in the school who had interacted with me a fair amount. So he knew that behind my complete detachment from the school and my classmates, there was no true reserve.

I've had the description "loner" applied to me, which actually describes me more than "reserved." A lot of people have sure thought so. (My older brother Dale, now deceased, always told people that because no one in the family knew where to find me, since I kept to myself so much, he was certain I worked for the CIA.)

Dan was responsible for my second favorite memory from my senior year, because he pulled a prank on me that the class executed for him during our graduation ceremony in June of 1970. We were all seated in the high school gymnasium, facing a stage erected on a platform, and we had to line up row by row to cross the stage and receive our diplomas before returning to our seats in the audience. When it was my turn to climb the few steps onto the stage and cross it, I suddenly became aware that the class was singing quite low, Elvis' "You Ain't Nothing But a Hound Dog." I came within a hair of whipping around to stare at the audience then double over laughing. I did start laughing, but I did not stop in my tracks to bend over and hold my stomach, which is what I almost did—and probably should have done and often wished afterwards that I had done because that would have made the situation even funnier by being even crazier and more unexpected. I have always thought it would have been absolutely hilarious to see the crowd trying to understand why that girl was staggering all over the stage and bellowing with laughter.

It was a funny prank, probably because it was so harmless (for all Dan's crazy sense of humor, I never saw him be mean), and I've never been able to remember it without automatically getting a big grin. When I sat down, the girl next to me—and, unfortunately, I do not recall who it was—whispered to me that Dan had put everyone up to this.

At the time, I knew Dan was just teasing me about liking Elvis—after all, in our senior class wills, I teased him first by willing him and Ned my collection of Elvis records—but five years later, in 1975, due to my liking for "old-time" 1930s black delta blues (such as Son House, Robert Johnson, and Lead Belly's "Goodnight Irene" and "Midnight Special"), which was the earliest music I consciously recall hearing, I took a college course in music that "decoded" the sexual content in old blues and R&B songs. (Everything in them was actually referring to sex in one way or another.) And I discovered that the phrase "you ain't nothing but a hound dog" actually meant "you ain't nothing but a m-f....er."

All those 1950s teenagers never had a clue what they were dancing to.

---

Many of my classmates knew Dan well all his life, but I did not. For me, he was the cute, crazy guy who, in 1970, sat in the back row of my high school English Literature class and made me laugh. By the time I moved back to the area where he still lived and we had attended high school together, Dan was a fond memory from nearly 50 years in our past. Then, for a couple of months during the fall of 2018, my path briefly crossed Dan's again after Ned got in touch with me about the upcoming reunion. A short-lived email correspondence ensued between Dan and me in which we talked about his time in the Navy and mine in the Air Force, and since Dan liked to laugh and make people laugh, I don't think he will mind if I share the following excerpts from our exchange that contain a few laughs about our years in the military.

**From Amy to Dan and Ned:**
Dan, I was joking with you about being able to spot Navy guys, so I thought you might enjoy a little story about an ex-Navy guy I ran across. Now, first I have to tell you that when I was in the Air Force I developed a dead-on instinct for knowing which branch of the service a man had served in even though he was in civilian clothes and/or had not been in the military for several years. I was so good at it that I was never wrong, although I've since lost the skill because I haven't used it for years.

Well, back in 1976, I was living in Columbus, and I had taken a job at the Ohio National Bank, working their evening/night shift in their computer division. I would get off work at about two a.m. and get home and be so wound up, I often did not get to sleep until about six a.m. That November I moved into a new apartment. Back then, a man had to come to your place to install the phone, and the appointment could be made only for the day, but not for the hour. Wouldn't you know, the guy showed up at eight a.m., right on the dot. Thus I had had maybe two hours of sleep before he came pounding on my door and dragging me out of a groggy slumber. I threw on a covering of some sort (I don't recall owning an actual robe), staggered to the door and yanked it open, and there stood a burly, bearded guy cheerily announcing that he had come to install my phone.

You'll have to picture this to get the full impact. Me—groggy from lack of sleep and all my body rhythms out of joint anyhow from the crazy hours (I lasted only six months in the night job before I found a day job to replace it), standing at my front door, staring at this man, not saying a single word because my brain would not function, let alone my tongue, and finally realizing I needed to bring him inside. So, still not saying a word I just thrust the door wide open and gestured for him to follow me. I led him into the bedroom and indicated by gesture—still no words—that I wanted the phone installed by the bedside table. Then I slumped down on the edge of my unmade bed, hung my head down, and stared at the floor.

I sat like that while he busied himself until the realization finally worked its way through my foggy brain that, although he was pretending to be cheerful, he was actually glancing warily at me out of the side of his eyes, and I knew he thought I was one weird girl. The awareness also dawned on me right then that in my silent refusal to speak a single word to him, I had been neither friendly nor courteous; therefore, perhaps I should exhibit some manners and interact with some friendly chitchat.

So, without looking up at him, still staring at the floor in my zombie condition, barely dressed with nothing on but some old shirt, my long hair hanging halfway down my back, all ragged and wild and tangled from rolling around in bed, I said in a slow, foghorn voice that was rough from no sleep: "You . . . look like . . . an ex-Navy man . . . to me."

That man literally, physically, jumped backwards away from me. He almost dropped the phone, which startled me so much that I finally looked up at him. His entire body was shaking, and his voice was trembling as he said, "HHHH-ooow-www did you know that?"

I was in such a zombie mental state that I could not form a reply. All I could do was just stare at him with glazed, uncomprehending eyes, which scared even more of the crap out of him, because he finished the phone in about thirty more seconds and ran for the door. I don't mean he walked fast or hastened. He ran out of that apartment.

He was already in his truck and peeling out of the parking lot by the time I got up, followed him to the front door, closed it—he had not shut it behind him after he jerked it wide-open and lunged through it—locked it, and got back in bed.

It was only later, after I had had some sleep and could think again, that I understood how funny it was. I did not have a chance to explain how I knew—that it was just my personal, ordinary experience in the military—partly because I was in no condition to explain and partly because he did not stay around long enough to hear.

**From Dan to Amy:**
Good writing, Amy. Tell me more.

**From Amy to Dan and Ned:**
More about the phone man, Dan? Never saw him again.

Or more about Navy men? Let's see, I was stationed in England for two years, so all I know about Navy guys is their affinity for the Ladies of the Night in Mediterranean ports, but you probably know more about that than I do.

Or just more funny stories? I do have another one that took place in Omaha. I don't have time to write it now, but if I get an hour free, I'll tell you about it.

**From Dan to Amy:**
You're just lucky you aren't here where I could get my hands on you. I would like to hear your stories about where you went in the service. When we went to different ports, I went to the nicest restaurants instead of chasing dirty women or drinking Budweiser. I can't wait until you get time to tell more. You are a good communicator.

**From Amy to Dan and Ned:**
Okay, Dan, I believe you. Uh huh, yeah, I'm sure you never had a single encounter with a Lady of the Night, just like all the other sailors I knew.

I spent my first year in Colorado—in Denver, then in Colorado Springs, which has tons of military bases. The Air Force Academy is in Colorado Springs along with an Army base (Fort Carson), Peterson Field (now Peterson AFB where I worked), Ent AFB (where I lived and which, I've been told, has since closed and is now an Olympic training center), and a place called Cheyenne Mountain, which is a hollowed-out mountain in the Rockies that houses NORAD (North American Aerospace Defense Command). From there I went to England for two years, and finally returned to the States, to SAC Headquarters (Strategic Air Command) at Offutt AFB in Omaha.

Then I got out and came back to Ohio, to Columbus and Ohio State University to major in journalism. Quit after 18 months, went to work, met Doug, returned to college, got degrees in journalism and art (painting, drawing), stopped just shy of getting another degree in art history. Racked up enough credits in political science that I probably could have finished one there had I wanted to, but I didn't. (I have a wide range of interests.)

I understand the nice restaurants though (if that's actually what you did in those ports—arggghh, get your hands off my throat, I believe you, I believe you), as I have a liking for those myself. Right after I got to England I started seeing this guy, and we were together for the two years we were there. (We're still friends, even now 45 years later; he's a retired drama teacher in Seattle.) He and I spent a weekend each month in London, attending plays, and we always included a nice dinner prior to the performance.

I still have the theatre booklets in pristine condition. I figure by the time I'm ready to die (I'm thinking I'll make it to a hundred) those should be worth a lot of money to collectors, so I'll have to pick one of my nieces to leave them to, since we have no children. Doug suggested the Midland Theatre might want them. I'll ask and if they do, they'll get them. Otherwise, I'll give them to someone to sell online.

The one thing Doug and I have missed after moving out here in Fallsburg in 2003 was the easy access to good restaurants. Initially we went to the Manna in Newark, but that closed. We also went to the Granville Inn, but that closed, although they've reopened, and we went to the Cherry Valley Lodge. Then they switched to a family oriented place, and call me a crotchety old lady, but I can't take the screaming kids when I'm trying to eat. It's just not the atmosphere I want to pay good money for. I'd rather stay home.

Hmmm, I just remembered something. I read a book by the Navy man who created SEAL Team Six, and I am certain he said Budweiser was their beer drink of choice. That you even *knew* that tells me something.

**From Dan to Amy:**
Fallsburg, home of the mushroom.

I went to Colorado a couple of years ago for my niece's wedding. It was indescribable. Certainly not what I had envisioned. I was mostly around the Denver area. I can't remember the name of the town, but it was real nice.

I always wanted to write about existentialism since I felt that topic to be neglected. As the years went by, I lost interest.

Not really lost interest, but just didn't feel like sharing anything. My military career consisted of four years in the Navy. I went in at 29. My dad was a B-17 pilot in WWII, and no one else in our family had done any military time. I felt I owed it to him. I wanted to join the Marines and kill people, but they couldn't offer a guarantee. Same with the Army and Air Force. The Navy guaranteed me sonar training or I would get an honorable discharge if they couldn't keep their obligation. I scored one point off a perfect score on the ASVAB, so they wanted to put me in nuclear school. I didn't fall for that. Spent four years as a Sonar Technician stationed in Long Beach, CA. I never let one communist bastard get past Las Vegas, so that's the closest they came to Newark, OH, while I was in. I was named Sailor of the Quarter and Sailor of the Year on the USS *Duncan* FFG-10, a guided missile frigate. Went to exotic places like San Diego and San Francisco. Oh yes, I can't forget Guam. I got out of the Navy and worked nine years as a private investigator in Los Angeles. Just like the old black-and-white movies I grew up with. I came back to Ohio and got licensed in this state only to be disappointed. Never made any money in three years. You can go to the barber shop and find out anything you want to know, plus get a haircut. I couldn't cut hair. Now, here I am waiting for the end. I just got a new car. They wanted to sell me one on a six-year loan. Ha. I'm 65. I got a three-year lease. I'm not buying it for my wife or my son; I'm buying it for me. Did you ever notice that most every naval base is near the water? I didn't break up anything into paragraphs because you didn't either. It's our secret way of communicating. The Park Place Bistro in Newark has pretty good food. It's where the Natoma was. Just in case you ever make it off the farm.

**From Amy to Dan and Ned:**

Thanks for the laughs. I broke my previous letter into many paragraphs. If it came to you in one chunk, it was not my fault as it had, by my count, nine paragraphs.

Doug has gone to bed early because he has to make a site visit tomorrow, Saturday, a rare workday for him, and I am sitting here with my cat, half watching *Ancient Aliens Declassified*, so I thought I would answer your letter. I used to think I wanted to see a UFO, then realized at some point that I don't want the aliens to know where to find me. I used to subscribe to *UFO Magazine*, but they stopped sending it and never sent me a renewal, so I think they either went out of business or switched to online only. They published some believable stuff, but some was not. I remember one article in particular where the guy was claiming he had seen all this secret alien/UFO stuff while in the Air Force, but, having been there myself, I found all kinds of holes in his story that sounded as if the closest he ever got to America's Air Force was seeing an American Airlines plane fly over his house.

[Dan: Did you ever notice that most every naval base is near the water?]

Yes, that has always baffled me, but do you want to hear something really crazy? They put Air Force bases on these wide-open plains, then cover the ground around them, for miles, with a layer of concrete. Just these huge, empty expanses of concrete. They call them "flight lines."

I had this coworker back in the 1980s who moved to St. Louis to be with her fiancé. While there she took a job with a private investigator. Ten months later she was back in Columbus, the wedding called off. She told me that her company dealt mostly with checking up on spouses or lovers to see if they were cheating, and she became so paranoid that her groom-to-be was cheating on her that she started checking up on him—going through his pockets, listening to his calls, following him. Apparently, he got tired of leaving work and finding her parked up the block watching him through binoculars and decided he couldn't marry that. I asked her if she found any evidence, and she said, not a trace, but that didn't mean it wasn't happening, and she just hadn't caught him. I told her she should find another line of work. There's such a thing as justified suspicions—then there's being totally bonkers.

[Dan: I went to Colorado a couple of years ago for my niece's wedding. It was indescribable. Certainly not what I had envisioned.]

You didn't explain what you meant by this. I was there in 1971, and returned briefly in 1974 (just before I left the Air Force) on a trip from Offutt to recover our computer data (by using the computer at the Air Force Academy). In 1971, the hippies were starting to take over the state, especially Colorado Springs, which I have always called "Hippie Haven." I loved Colorado. But, it's my understanding the hippies have drastically altered it during the past 45 years. I was not surprised when the state legalized marijuana, as I was always the only person in the room at every party I ever attended in Colorado

Springs who did not smoke, drink, or do drugs. The guy I was involved with did not touch drugs either, but he did drink and smoke. I got along with the potheads though because— and this is the truth, not a joke—they told me they were try- ing to get their minds, via drugs, where mine was naturally.

I was in California in 1973. I came back to the States with the guy I was involved with in England to visit his fam- ily in Seattle. He had grown up in L.A., in Anaheim, next to Disneyland. We took a car trip from Seattle down to L.A. and back up. We stopped off briefly in San Francisco. Mostly he wanted to show me where he had grown up and take me to Disneyland. I confess I intensely disliked Los Angeles and could not wait to shed that city. I have never seen so many skinny, over-tanned, bitchy women before or since. The atmosphere in that city was just awful, and as we drove away, I could feel the negativity fading from the air the farther we got on the highway. I have never had any desire to return.

I do like detective stories, though, and murder mysteries in books or movies. In fact, I cut my adult reading teeth, when I was eleven, on Agatha Christie and Erle Stanley Gardner books. My older sister read them and passed them along. I don't have much time for it now, but once in a while I'll read one. I'm going to have to find time to write you and Ned my Omaha War Story.

---

A full year went by after the above brief exchange with Dan, and during that year I was so busy trying to bring my first book

(*Aries: Doorway to Initiation*) into print that I never found time to write that Omaha story or exchange any more emails with Dan. One year later, on November 22, 2019, Ned sent me an email announcing Dan's passing, accompanied by a copy of his obituary, which included the following highlights that I have extracted and condensed in order to give readers a taste of his personality:

> Dan attended Ohio University, studying communications, before joining WCLT Radio as an on-air personality where he enjoyed playing songs not on the approved playlist, sharing behind-the-scenes information regarding popular music, and using his ready wit to keep Licking County drivers laughing out loud. He met his wife, Sherry, at WCLT. He was a proud father of his son Cliff, and he amazed and delighted his friends and family with his spectacular, beautifully prepared meals, his cheesecake, grilled ribs, and homegrown tomatoes. He leaves his family feeling the hollowness of loss. If there is a golf course in the Afterlife, Dan will be landing a long drive on the green and easily stroking it in with a grin. "Birdied it," he'll say with a satisfied chuckle.

When I was writing to Dan, a year before his death, I had not known how ill he was, but afterwards, rereading his emails, I found that poignant line—"Now, here I am waiting for the end."

I had thought Dan was simply joking about the fact that we were all so much older, closing in on 70, but he wasn't. He knew his end on this earth was coming very quickly, and he would soon be leaving this dimension for the next one. Yet he was still laughing and taking the time to make me laugh. I spent a few days regretting that I never wrote and sent the stories he had asked for, just to make him laugh at a point in his life when he surely needed laughter, the way he had made me laugh at a point in my life when I had needed laughter. But in my state of regret, over-shadowed by my knowledge that the soul is eternal, I decided to tell Dan the story of Omaha anyhow, to write down all the stories he had asked me for, the stories I had said I would send him when I had more time, not realizing that of the two of us, it was Dan who did not have more time.

# Chapter 2

# My Omaha Story

In February 1974, the Air Force transferred me from England to Offutt AFB, SAC HQS, in Omaha, Nebraska. I had nine months left in the Air Force, which I intended to spend (and I did spend) planning a smooth transition back to civilian life. Although I had enjoyed my years in the military, I had no desire to stay.

I had come to Offutt from a base that had fewer than 50 enlisted women on it, half of whom lived off base. The rest of us lived in quiet harmony on the top floor of a large dormitory. I had lived in a private room while stationed in England, and, in fact, I had happily enjoyed a private room during most of my previous three years of service. Any roommate assigned to me rarely lasted long for one reason or another. In contrast, the WAF dorm at Offutt was terribly overcrowded because one of the two dorms was being renovated, and all its residents had been crowded into the remaining dorm. The noisy, acrimonious atmosphere in the overcrowded dorm was tangible enough that it hit me as a physical blow the first moment I lugged my suitcases past the entrance, dropped them on the floor in an empty community room, and stood there, almost reeling from the surging currents of animosity in the very air and wondering just exactly what hell I had been sent to. The hostile situation was heightened for me personally because I was assigned to a room containing a white girl who was a pathological liar, a compulsive troublemaker, and the most racist bigot I have encountered in this lifetime. She devoted every moment of her existence to producing enough racial division between the black and white girls to make a Klan member proud, and she was remarkably successful at it because she hid her malice behind a pretense of sweet innocence.

I withstood my roommate's ignorance for about a month, staying silent and withdrawn, commenting on nothing she said or did, cultivating a neutral facial expression that never conveyed my thoughts, until finally, the tamped-down pressure blew out of me one evening in reaction to one of her venomous tirades against the black race. I knew, even as I exploded, that I now needed to move out of her room and the dorm itself as quickly as possible and get as far from her as I could get, because now that she realized I was not the passive, easily manipulated puppet that she had mistakenly thought I was, she was going to start lying about me, and I had seen her in action enough to know that she would tell any conceivable lie to exact her revenge.

Without giving my roommate one hint of warning as to my intentions (to ensure she could not launch her vicious attacks before I was gone and thereby instigate potential problems for me with my fellow dorm mates or, even worse, our WAF Commander), I immediately and secretly sought the aid of another WAF named Mary, from Wisconsin, who also desperately wanted out of the emotionally and mentally destructive atmosphere. The two of us rented an apartment off base and departed that dormitory as hastily as circumstances allowed.

Mary had been at Offutt much longer than I had, and she not only knew my roommate was the source of the racial tension, but also she had tried to convey as much to our First Sergeant with zero results. I never attempted that. In the mere four weeks I had been on the base, I had many times witnessed that First Sergeant and my roommate together in my dorm room, mutually lamenting the inability of my perfect, sweet, sainted roommate to resolve the hostile conflicts in the dorm "no matter how hard she tried," and I knew our First Sergeant had her head so far up my roommate's rear that she was incapable of seeing anything but my roommate's shit. So, I left with Mary before my roommate's malicious lies could turn that First Sergeant's wrath onto me.

By splitting expenses, Mary and I were able to afford a pleasing, furnished, two-bedroom, two-bathroom apartment that included a balcony off the dining room. Mary was a bit of a fanatic about sanitation; therefore, although the apartment was clean, before we moved in Mary insisted we spend a day sanitizing everything to suit her much higher standards. She even sprayed our mattresses with Lysol, which was not the greatest idea Mary ever had for me. We learned too late that I was allergic to the Lysol after I woke the next morning covered with an itchy rash that had crept off the mattress and straight through the sheets onto my skin while I slept contentedly unaware of this sneaky chemical attack.

On the day we sanitized the apartment, Mary tackled the mattresses and dressers in the bedrooms while I washed the windows. When I started on the glass doors leading to the balcony, I discovered an odd yellow substance streaking their exterior. I could not determine what it was or what had produced it, nor could Mary after I called her outside for a second opinion. We puzzled over it and speculated various possibilities, because neither of us had ever seen its like, but since it washed off easily, we shrugged and dismissed it as most likely some form of plant sap that had blown against the glass.

We moved in, and soon afterwards we were both home one day—she was in the combination kitchen/dining room and I was in my bedroom—when I heard an undefined racket accompanied by a gigantic gush of water. Since any unexpected torrent of water running loose within a house or an apartment usually means a water pipe has broken, I leaped to my feet to go help restrain the flood with duct tape and towels, but in that same moment, Mary abruptly hollered at the top of her lungs: "That damn woman! That goddamn filthy woman! That's filthy!"

I had barely made it into the living room—which, in this two-bedroom flat, was only four short steps from my bedroom door—when Mary plunged past me like an Olympic sprinter, slammed the door open, still hollering, "That goddamn filthy woman! That's filthy!" and exited the apartment into the building's foyer, leaving our door bouncing and swinging in her rush to get wherever she was going.

The outside entrance into our building opened into a spacious foyer, off which were four apartments (ours being one), and in the center of the foyer was a staircase about six feet wide that curved up to the second floor. The staircase was completely open, not enclosed with walls, just bordered with railings. Even the steps themselves were open. Consequently, I could hear Mary yelling and cussing all the way up those stairs, which she was leaping two at a time, and when she arrived at the top, she commenced pounding on the door to the apartment directly above us, hollering: "Damn you! You open this door, you filthy woman."

Mary had whipped out of our apartment and bolted up the stairs so rapidly that I was still standing in flat-footed bewilderment in the center of our living room, groping mentally to comprehend what she was doing and why she was doing it. Mary had spent her youth in apartment complexes, in somewhat low-income housing, but this was my first time living in an apartment of any kind. I did not have her experience with . . . let's tactfully call it . . . the wide variety of people who inhabit apartment complexes. She had known instantly what was happening the very second she heard the racket and the accompanying gush of water, whereas I still had no clue, despite standing only about six feet from both sounds.

So, I pivoted in place and followed the noise over to the dining area where I halted, gape-mouthed, to gaze out the glass doors (which, fortunately, were tightly closed) and up at the balcony above ours in near awe of an impossible scene. The woman who lived directly above us had sent her three large dogs out on her balcony to pee, but the balconies had slatted floors with extra wide gaps between the boards, and a splendid deluge of dog piss was raining down onto our balcony and splashing all over our glass doors—clearing up our questions as to the nature and source of the mysterious yellow substance.

Those dogs must have stored it up for a couple of days, because this was a hurricane of piss, and the moment of its release had been eagerly anticipated by all three dogs, for they were enthusiastically barking and pissing and joyously tussling each other in lively friendliness for the best position to take aim at our doors.

I honestly stared straight up at this for several seconds before I was able to comprehend the situation, because I could not wrap my brain around the reality of *anyone* residing in a non-Third World nation, where the population is fully cognizant of the latest developments in sanitation, doing what I was so clearly seeing. Despite being only 21 years old, I still had enough life experience under my belt to know that it was my destiny to have the dumbest people on this earth inflicted onto me. This woman, however, was a surprising marvel of stunning stupidity—although, to give her the respect she deserves, she was carrying out that time-honored tradition of siccing the dogs on people in a phenomenally creative way.

Don't get me wrong. I was not totally unfamiliar with public urination. After all, I had lived the first 10 years of my life in the remote woods where there wasn't another house for a good mile, and when my brother Randy and I were out stirring up the water snakes in our creek, we did not regard needing the toilet as a compelling reason to return to the house when we could more easily deposit our unwanted fluids behind handy bushes and trees. Yet our youth and lack of sophistication did not prevent us from knowing we were supposed to disappear behind separate bushes for a while and not squat over each other's heads. Our mother may not have been to the manor born, but she was definitely to the manners born, and urinating on someone's head would never have crossed her mind—or, for that matter, the mind of anyone I had ever met, heard of, or read about. Thus my slow-witted grasp that this unique downpour was the brainstorm of a fellow adult human was not a mental deficiency on my part, just a direct consequence of a mother who regarded manners as a required asset.

By the time Mary returned, furious, red-faced, and still cussing, my delayed comprehension had caught up with me, and I was on the sofa, all cramped up from laughing at what had almost happened—the two of us sitting on that balcony, enjoying a morning cup of tea, and suddenly being drenched with dog piss and clobbered with big sloshy turds.

Mary, at that time, had no sense of humor for the absurdities in life or the lunacies of people, though she later developed one from being around me. She did *not* see what was so funny, even when I began crooning: "Dog piss is falling on my head, that dog piss keeps falling, so I just did me some cussing at the woman and said I don't like the way you get things done . . ."

(A parody of a 1960s song composed by Burt Bacharach and Hal David: "Raindrops Keep Falling On My Head . . . those raindrops keep falling, so I just did me some talking to the sun . . .")

Being young and naïve about the ways of the world, Mary and I knew exactly how to take care of the matter. We confidently hastened to the manager and reported the incident, righteously anticipating his shock and dismay and immediate willingness to remedy the situation on our behalf. He told us that her dogs were free to piss on our heads because she was a permanent, long-term resident and we were transients who would be there for only eight months. (I was being discharged in eight months, and Mary was planning to move to a less expensive, single bedroom unit in another area.) The manager was genuinely perplexed as to how we could regard this incident as unacceptable uncleanness, and he dismissed us as whiny, halfway stupid brats who were abusing his time and patience with a ridiculous complaint, equivalent to spotting a speck of dirt on the ground where dirt is obviously going to be located.

It took Mary and me a full bewildering day to grasp that we were not just living underneath a World Champion moron, we were also renting from someone who did not have even that much discernible brain activity. Together, they formed an unassailable wall of stupidity. Even worse, they ruled our small universe, and they were pissing all over it and not even bothering to bring along a container of Lysol.

Two unsanitary idiots, unable to recognize a bottle of disinfectant, were two more than what Mary had room for in her life. With her jaw locked grimly in place and her hands determined to carry a battle banner for Lysol, she raised such a ruckus that after a few days of hearing it, the manager told the woman she had to take her dogs for a walk every time they felt a joyous desire to stake out our balcony as their personal territory.

For the remaining months that we lived there, the woman complied, but I bet Mary a thousand dollars that the second we moved out, that woman released those dogs onto the balcony once again.

# Chapter 3

# The Cardboard Box Affair

Except for the woman in Omaha, I've had tolerable neighbors even during close-quarter living in apartment complexes. Most of the time we left each other alone, and, on my part, I can think of only one time that I thought leaving someone alone was a bad idea.

I was 25 and renting a second-floor flat in a two-story apartment building. The unit directly beneath mine was empty for most of the three years that I lived there, but at some point a lone man in his forties, who I suspect was on a temporary work assignment to our city, occupied it for a few months. One early evening, the most hellacious groaning and painful howling began filtering up through the floor from his apartment into mine. I ignored it at first, but his tormented screeching continued, periodically varying in both volume and distress yet never pausing for even one second, and in my concern that he needed help, I several times stretched out on the floor and pressed my ear tight against it in an effort to understand what I was hearing. I was not being nosy. My concern was quite validly based upon a friend who, upon being attacked and raped in her apartment in that exact same complex, had screamed continually in the hope that the person living above her would hear and call the police.

An hour of these wretched groans passed while my apprehension increased and I paced my apartment, worried that he had injured himself, or he was undergoing a stroke or a heart attack, or an intruder was attacking him and he was hoping I heard and called for help.

Every few minutes I stopped pacing long enough to shove my ear against the floor, trying to hear something that would enable me to choose between helping or not helping. Having never met or even nodded hello to this man, I could not guess how he might react should I start rapping on his door, but finally, I grabbed my shoes and was busy tugging them on when his tortured howls abruptly halted. I waited, my ears straining in alarm that he had died as a consequence of my vacillation. I dropped down again and thrust my ear hard against the floor and heard the faint murmur of a woman's voice. I sat up slowly, carefully placed my shoes aside, and leaned back for a long while, awed by the level and length of his excitement, but immeasurably relieved that I had not nosed where I was not wanted.

Shortly after that incident I met Doug, we moved across town, and I continued to live in peaceful coexistence with my neighbors for the next few years. Then, one turbulent day, quite unexpectedly, I ran up against a neighbor so ignorant and rude that he made the Omaha woman who dispatched her dogs to pee on our heads look like the pinnacle of highbrow intelligence and Victorian era manners.

This piece of bad news was a "neighbor" only because he owned the rental property, a condominium, across the street from us when we were living in the Upper Arlington suburb of Columbus, Ohio. He warrants an entire chapter, however, because he was living, breathing proof that stupidity can show up anywhere, under any circumstances, if given half a chance.

One August night, a horrifically destructive wind, rain and electrical storm took down, on our street alone, about 50 large trees, just broke them in two about halfway up. By early morning, these broken trees cluttered every street, yard, and sidewalk, and the city's cleanup crew—burly men with cranes, roaring chainsaws, and monster trucks that chewed the smaller debris into mulch—was swarming the street as soon as the storm ended. Most of the trees were anywhere from 18 to 36 inches in diameter, and they were dangerously and precariously arranged because their upper halves had snapped off and dropped down to lean against their lower halves. To safely clear this mess, the men had to chop each broken half into manageable chunks then take the rest of the tree down too, if they could not save it.

The morning following the storm was also our recyclable pickup day. Those of us who lived on my side of the street routinely placed our recyclables with those on the curb across the street so that the pickup men could make a clean sweep down the street, conveniently clearing only one side and saving themselves work, energy, and time by not having to crisscross the street. I would not have recycled anything that morning in order to keep obstacles out of the cleanup crew's way, but I needed to clear a stack of flattened cardboard boxes from the bed of Doug's pickup truck so that we could load a new queen mattress into it the next evening and deliver it to our newly built art studio way out in the country on the land where we now live.

When I arrived to deposit my cardboard, a man who was directing the cleanup of a huge tree in the front yard of one of the condominiums about two units down the street began shouting at me not to leave my boxes because "they won't pick that up."

I happened to be in an early morning state of total mental detachment from the world, so, although I called back an answer, I did so in a completely disinterested tone: "Yes, they will. They take corrugated cardboard."

The man reacted with a livid rage and instantly abandoned his task and came barreling across the yard and down the sidewalk—literally running at me full-speed as if chasing a pickpocket who had swiped his wallet—to engage me in a conversation that was so *stupid* you will think I made it up.

When he came hurtling toward me, repeatedly and aggressively hollering at me not to place my cardboard there, I instinctively knew he was viewing this as a heaven-sent opportunity to instigate a fight that he mistakenly thought would make him look important in front of his cleanup crew; but in my disinterested and detached mental state, his motivations and actions were so ridiculous that when he finally pulled up beside me to berate me for "putting trash outside," I was barely seeing him, not in an avoiding way, just with indifference. Still, I managed to reply that it was recycling day, to gesture at all the other recyclables, and to add that we had all been doing this for at least 10 years.

He then said I had no right to put my recyclables on the curb because I did not own the property—which I immediately recognized as his reason for charging at me like some maddened rhino. He wanted me to know that he was a Hotshot Landlord, wealthy enough to own expensive rental property in an expensive neighborhood.

My absorbed interest in the cleanup activities and my silent, unspeaking indifference to his personal importance enraged him, and he began repeatedly saying that because I did not own the strip of land between the street and the sidewalk (thus implying that he owned it), I had no right to place recyclables on it. I knew the city owned it along with a certain number of feet back from the curb, but all I said—in a tone so bored I did not bother to raise my voice—was: "You are being unintelligent. Placing our recyclables on the curb for a couple of hours during one day of the week is not an important issue."

He bellowed that it was important because of "cosmetic appearances" and I should put mine on my side of the street to "spread it around."

Since I did not—and still do not—speak Stupid, I was unable to reply to his statement that attractive landscaping required spreading trash in as many directions as possible. I also did not bother to switch my attention off the cleanup crew to even glance in his direction, and my lack of response incensed him. In an effort to force me to react with anger equal to his own, he assumed a phony tone of "pointed" condescension and said: "Well, you've *informed* me of something today. You've really *taught* me something. I didn't *know* this."

I simply continued my silent vigil on the workers and their methods for carefully dismantling those huge and dangerously positioned trees. Doug and I had dead trees on our country property that we were planning to take down (or have someone else take down for us), and I wanted to know how it was safely done.

The Hotshot Landlord suddenly decided that he was also a Hotshot Lawyer, driven by a passionate need to address all recycling aberrations with extensive legal remedies. He hoisted himself into an imperious puffball and demanded: "Well, just what are the city regulations that allow this? Do you have any laws to back you up?"

I personally thought that any introduction of laws into our interactions should include one that allowed me to whack him upside the head with a chunk of my cardboard; but, instead of saying so, I emerged from my disinterested silence long enough to shrug indifferently and tell him, without taking my eyes off the workers, "I have no idea. It's just the way we have always done it."

"Well, I'm going to check into it," he threatened, then waited expectantly for me to blanch and tremble all over in fear of zoning laws and codes descending on me. All I did was indifferently indicate, by turning to leave, that I was finished listening to him, which is when our exchange entered the realm of total idiocy.

He abruptly pointed at the huge, now broken tree, *growing* in his front yard, the same one the storm had snapped in half, the same one that large, husky workmen were preparing to take down with chainsaws and cranes, and he told me in a hostile, autocratic tone that he did not want to see me putting any more of those in his yard.

Now, this was a *tree*—not a few broken branches, but a full-grown, 2,000 pound *tree*, with roots reaching halfway to the center of the earth because this tree had been there long before I ever moved to that street, and I had lived there for 18 years. The wind had split this monster tree into separate pieces approximately halfway up its trunk—and he was now accusing me of personally planting that tree in his yard then returning three decades later and breaking it in two with my bare hands.

Just for the record—not that you can't figure it out for yourself—he was not making finely tuned accusations, worthy of logical debate. So, still without bothering to look at him, while using the same dismissive tone I had been using, I pointed out the obvious: "I had nothing to do with putting that tree in your yard or its demise."

He backtracked, enthusiastically fumbled through his brain for something even more ludicrous that he could say, and found it when he dragged out: "That's not what I meant to say. I meant that I don't want you putting any of these *other* trees in my yard," and he gestured at the broken trees filling the street and scattered along its sides.

Again, these were *trees*. TREES. Not thin, two-foot long broken branches off trees, but actual downed *trees* of a height and diameter that several strong, brawny men could not lift. The city's cleanup crew was using cranes and harnesses to climb into the trees that were partially standing, and they were using chainsaws big enough to take down a redwood to slice the fallen trees into manageable pieces that could be transferred onto trucks.

Yet, somehow, I, a woman, who was at that time in my early forties, standing five feet, five inches and weighing 125 pounds, was going to march along the street, lazily reach down and lightly heft 900 pound, 40-foot-long tree trunks onto my shoulders—one log per shoulder, each log at least 18 to 36 inches in diameter, and each log dragging dozens of large limbs—stroll over, and for some inexplicable reason known only to his unintelligent mind, casually deposit them in his yard before going back for more.

It occurred to me then that someday this man would quite possibly win a Darwin Award. (For those of you who are unfamiliar with the Darwin Awards, it's a mock award, begun by a woman named Wendy Northcutt and given to people who improve the human gene pool by "removing themselves from it in a spectacularly stupid manner" to quote directly from her book. Look them up on the internet. The award-winning stories are hilarious accounts of human stupidity, and the asides are equally funny. One of my favorites is: "The difference between genius and idiocy? Genius has its limits.")

His bizarre implication that I could effortlessly sweep huge fallen trees into the equivalent of a kitchen dustpan and discard them in his yard had only one reasonable reply possible, and I voiced it in my now well-practiced tone of dismissive indifference: "I have nothing to do with the cleanup."

At this point, the situation almost went completely south when he suddenly made the most ill-considered move he could have made. He grabbed at my arm, brushing across my wrist. I instantly stepped out of his reach and swung to face him, but my movement, despite its near invisible speed, was so smooth and natural, and my attitude so distant and detached, that he never realized he was within one more grab of hitting that sidewalk. Although it had been a few years since I had been in the dojo, training five to seven days per week and up to four hours per day (against men), I still privately practiced the kicks, and in the same second that my body realized it was in possible danger, it slid automatically and unconsciously into an offensive position. My one leg was slightly behind me, and I moved only far enough away to step into a kick to his crotch, which he never would have seen coming, for in his arrogant certainty that he could dominate my seeming passivity, he never suspected I even had such a skill.

Yet all I said, still in my detached mode, was: "I am not going to stand here and argue with you."

He said belligerently, "Oh yes, you *are* arguing. You're telling me I'm wrong."

I said calmly, "No, I'm telling you that you are unintelligent."

I began walking away.

He shouted after me that he was "going to check up on this."

I continued walking while I said over my shoulder in the indifferent tone of making an indifferent statement of fact: "You may do anything you wish, but you are unintelligent."

The moment I was past my front door, I called the appropriate government office to confirm my legal right to place my recyclables there, but I called only because I knew the man would call the same department for no other reason except to ensure that all city officials were fully aware of his personal importance. I declined to mention the arm grabbing and just calmly told the official that I had been dragged into an unintelligent, petty and absurd situation, so stupid that I did not want to waste one moment on it, but I had to because I had been accosted by a man who claimed I had no legal right to place my cardboard on "his" curb, and when I ignored him, he accused me of tearing down all the trees that the storm had felled, hauling them over, and pitching them into his yard. I needed to know my legal rights because the man was so aggressive that he might come pounding on my door.

A reasonable and calm official said that as far as he knew I could put my recyclables there, but for confirmation I could call Development for the codes. Just a few minutes after I hung up, Doug called, heard my story, and instantly assessed the neighbor man's motivation the same way I had—that he was using intimidation and his ownership of property in an upscale neighborhood to try to impress me that he was a wealthy, important, and powerful person.

When I told Doug, who, as an architect, had spent years dealing with the city's Building Department, that I had been advised to call Development, he laughed and said, "Then that's exactly what you should do because I know all those people in Development. I've worked with all of them. Call (so and so) and tell her that I gave you her name."

I did not bother with more calls. I just continued putting my recyclables in the exact same spot, and I never saw or heard from that man again.

I'm guessing that in the years since our little dustup, the city workers have referred to any meaningless, stupid incident as Another Cardboard Box Affair, and when anyone asks how it got that name, someone says: "Well, the story goes that about 20 years ago, some landlord ordered this woman to place her cardboard boxes on her side of the street for recycling, and when she ignored him, he accused her of tearing down, with her bare hands, all the huge, full-grown trees along that street and dumping them in his yard . . ."

# Chapter 4
# Sailors and Seasickness

**I never thought to ask Dan** if he ever got an opportunity to enjoy the pleasure of being seasick, nor did I tell him that I can never think of the Navy without thinking of when I was just past 19, in March 1972, and a friend and I took a ferry across the English Channel to Holland. The sea was rough, and Paul and I got hideously, unrelentingly seasick.

I had never before sailed on a larger body of water than the Ohio River, which, because it's a river, flows in only one general direction unless it floods, but even then, unlike an ocean, the Ohio has the good sense just to spread itself out and not thrash around in simultaneous multiple directions as though having a seizure.

Because I had never before been seasick, I had not the vaguest idea how to relieve my misery, and let me say that a raging bout of seasickness is stomach nausea unequaled. It takes grand prize in all stomach sickness I have ever had, and I once got food poisoning off mushrooms, threw up for three days, and lost 15 pounds from the ordeal.

The ferry's lounge was a huge room, containing only a handful of people (all other passengers were chowing down in the restaurant) and a generous and convenient distribution of tall, metal, barrel-shaped wastebaskets, all of which were lined with heavy plastic bags and none of which was covered with a lid that might discourage use. Someone clearly understood that public vehicles transporting large numbers of people required plenty of trash receptacles capable of holding a great deal of refuse.

Paul and I seated ourselves in the lounge, eagerly anticipating engaging in some people watching, our favorite nosy pastime when in public places, but the ferry had barely departed on its swooping journey across the tops and along the bottoms of mountainous waves before both of us were huddled in our seats, oblivious to our surroundings, only partially aware of each other, and deep in search of a Zen state of mind that would mitigate the nausea spreading rapidly from our stomachs throughout every cell in our bodies.

Paul dealt with it by retreating fully inside himself, shutting his eyes, and sitting stone still, as if waiting for the nausea to evaporate, condense, and drop over the railing and back into the sea from whence it had come.

I dealt with it by staring blankly at the air in between periodically leaping to my feet and frantically rushing off to the toilet every time I could feel the vomit rising—which was about every five minutes, the length of time it took me to make a round trip to the toilet. The vomit kept promising to rise all the way to the surface, just to slide back down the moment I reached the toilet, which kept me sprinting back and forth at a steady, repetitious clip with no beneficial results.

In the course of this, despite my preoccupation with my unhappy stomach, I nonetheless noticed an attractive man, slender, quiet, slightly French-looking, perhaps in his forties, who was watching me. I thought nothing of it and was in no condition to ponder the matter anyhow. I was 19, had long, wavy, chestnut hair, a nice face, a slender shape, great legs. I was accustomed to male attention even from married men who were, as he was, obviously seated with his wife and children. Yet he was keeping a watchful eye on me, which I noticed because every five minutes I darted by him, twice, during my round-trips to the toilet in my futile effort to persuade my stubborn stomach to regurgitate its contents.

I had made probably 20 trips past him (10 round trips) when he stopped me quite courteously and said so gently and compassionately, "Eat some dry bread or some crackers. It will help."

I paused long enough to gaze down at him in his seat and catch his words, but in my bleary, nauseated confusion I did not understand why he was so keen to converse about food, which, I assure you, was the *last* thing I wanted to even think about, let alone discuss or, God help me, eat. Furthermore, as astonishing as it might seem, I honestly thought I was concealing how sick I was. In my youthful naiveté—and because I had not yet heaved my entire interior onto the floor of that lounge—I thought I was acquitting myself with the utmost of gracious discretion. The reality so vividly apparent to everyone else (that my multiple trips to the toilet were sufficient evidence that something dreadful was wrong with me) just zoomed right past me.

He quickly realized that I was too mentally frazzled by my unfulfilled yearning to vomit to even consider the usefulness of scoffing a few crackers, so he added: "Please. Believe me. Eat some dry bread. I used to be in the Navy. I know."

Some part of my brain distantly recalled reading about or hearing accounts of sailors eating crackers to ward off seasickness, but as blinded as I was by nausea, I could not have found that ferry's restaurant had he picked me up and carried me to it. Besides, I knew my body, and I was certain I was too far gone for anything to help me except a long, dedicated bout of vomiting. The crackers or bread might have helped Paul, but I have always been well-attuned to what my body needs to heal itself, and it was telling me: "No crackers. No bread. No food. Just let me puke."

I nodded at the sailor, mumbled a ragged thank you, and staggered back to my seat beside Paul where I huddled, so desperate for relief that I was willing to try Paul's approach, which is when I learned (and years later, it's still true) that any time I have to vomit, sitting with my eyes closed causes my body to relax and feel that it's whirling violently in place, as if strapped into one of those cheap carnival rides whose only purpose is to make you dizzy enough to throw up your corn dogs.

Within one minute, my spinning stomach gave one last groaning roll and brought the vomit up with it. I felt its relentless determination to erupt out of me past any intention or desire on my part to restrain it until I could reach a private receptacle, and I knew without one doubt that as near as that toilet was, I was never going to make it. Although I am completely incapable of shame for the natural functions of the human body, and I am way too practical to be embarrassed by bodily functions brought on by illness, even the pseudo-illness of puking in reaction to a rough sea, still, splattering vomit all over the floor, the furniture, and the legs of strangers was a most undignified and ungracious thing to do—and I did not want to do it.

So, in wild-eyed desperation, I glanced around the room in search of *anything* I could vomit into—a bowl, a bag, a planter— *anything* other than the floor, and I had only about four seconds to find that anything and get to it.

And that's when I saw the supreme wisdom of—the reason for—some ferry captain's generous distribution of large, four-foot high, three-foot diameter metal trashcans, all of them without one single, gleaming, interfering lid.

Right straight down the empty row of seats I was sitting in, but behind the seats, was a huge, open trash barrel, lined with a heavy-duty plastic bag, capable of holding a great deal of vomit without ever splitting open. The seats were plastic—probably so the crew could easily hose the place down after every trip—and they were bolted to the floor in a single, straight line; thus I had a clear path to the trash can that did not require me to stumble through a maze of shifting chairs and trip over the feet of a crowd of irritated people.

The one slight problem was that not only was the barrel situated behind the row of seats I was in, thereby forcing me to lean over the back of the seat to reach it, but also the only other occupant of that row of seats was a rather large, bulky, chunky man who was slumped in the chair exactly in front of that barrel.

In other words, even if I got there in time, he was in my way.

Now, I've always been physically quick, and back in those days I was training every day in the martial arts and my reflexes were extremely fast. So I was on my feet and down to that trash can in the half second my stomach was giving me to get there, and in one continuous motion—no Olympic ice skater gliding across the rink at 30 miles per hour could have slid more smoothly or skillfully or gracefully—I slid into the plastic chair beside that man, reared up on my knees, grabbed his shoulder to leverage myself high enough to shoot vomit over it without getting it on him, and puked directly past his ear into that barrel.

Unknown to me, he had been sitting so perfectly still, not moving a muscle, his chin resting on his chest, because he was in the same shape I was in, and he was secretly hiding a plastic barf bag in his hands, just waiting for a reason to use it, which arrived when I skidded up against him, clutched his shoulder, and heaved over it into that barrel.

He groaned, "Ohhhhhh-uggghhhhhh-gahhhhgggg . . ." lurched forward, and spewed vomit in the opposite direction from me, straight into the barf bag in his hand.

When he leaned forward, I instantly squeezed in behind him on his chair to give myself a better shot at the barrel, and for about five minutes the two of us sat folded around each other, heaving repeatedly in opposing directions like some kind of two-spouted vomit fountain.

I, cognizant of the manners my mother had instilled in me, began apologizing to him in between each of my heaves: "I'm so sorry (uggghhhhhh-gahhhhgggg) oh sir (uggghhhhhh-gahhhhg-ggg) I'm so sorry (uggghhhhhh-gahhhhgggg) please (uggghhhh-hh-gahhhhgggg) I do so apologize (uggghhhhhh-gahhhhgggg) . . ."

He groaned and gagged quite intensely. Whether he heard or even understood me (whether he spoke English or one of the European languages), I did not know. As far as I could tell, he didn't give a crap what I was saying, no matter what language I

40

said it in, and I was in no shape to determine whether any of his many different retching sounds were actual words from any recognizable language. Eventually I made one final heave, followed by one final extended apology, then departed for the toilet (past the sailor once again) to wash out my mouth.

Now that my stomach had what it wanted, I felt reasonably better, which enabled me to go sit down and engage myself in the task of pretending it had never happened. Whatever sheen of continental sophistication I might have projected had been wiped away, but I took a special pride in knowing that my bodily contents did not end up soaking the floor or splashed against anyone's legs.

As a postscript, that sailor knew what he was talking about. When Paul and I left the continent for the return trip, I bought a large loaf of bread in Amsterdam, and we each ate half of it before getting on the ferry. Neither of us underwent the slightest seasickness, and we even visited the ferry's restaurant and succumbed to a hearty and pleasing meal of roast chicken and vegetables. I recall nothing else about the ferry itself on the trip over or back. The human mind makes its own choices as to what it wishes to retain across the years of our lives, and for me, 50 years later, the images imprinted on my memory are that row of plastic seats, bolted to the floor, the bulky man seated in front of that barrel—and the sailor's face.

A few years later I met Doug and passed on the sailor's advice. Doug and his father often went fishing together on Lake Erie, and before launching they took pills to prevent seasickness. Yet Doug still got seasick, and worse, the pill itself made him sick. I told him to ditch the pill and eat plenty of dry bread of a good, hearty quality before he ever set sail. Doug thought something so simple could not possibly work, but after some persuasion, he tried it, and to his happy surprise he never had to take another seasick pill.

# Chapter 5
# Always Take Provisions

**My body has always had an instinct** for the foods it needs or the ones that will harm it. When I was a child and my brother ate luncheon meat sandwiches and my sister wanted peanut butter and jelly, I chose cheese and lettuce or cucumber and tomato. Even when I was hungry, I automatically rejected sweets in favor of nourishing fruits, vegetables, and protein-filled foods. I desired sweets only if I were not physically hungry. The only "wrong" food my body has ever craved is chocolate in response to that near universal female desire that occurs during one week out of every month when some women—though I won't name names—have considered murdering their sisters just for their chocolate bars. (That craving may not actually be "wrong." I read somewhere, decades ago, that chocolate causes blood to coagulate. If that's true, it might explain the mindless desire for chocolate that dominates the female physical body just prior to its monthly issue.)

My body has always had an equally developed instinct for medicines that will or will not help it, and since the doctors

I've known have been severely deficient in their ability to accurately diagnose my body, and I lack a sense of smell that will enable me to determine if food is spoiled, out of sheer self-preservation, I learned early in life to rely on my body's instinctual ability to advise me as to what foods and medicines I should ingest.

In June of 1972, I was 19 and in England, and some friends and I attended an outdoor rock concert at the Crystal Palace Bowl, a park in London that contained a little lake just in front of a domed performance area. An internet site has some pictures and a description of that concert—though not a lot of either, quite possibly because too many attendees were too stoned to ever remember having been there. I searched the online pictures to see if the camera had captured our group, but all I found was a posted comment from some British guy who said he was right behind a group of Americans, which sounded hopeful until he further stated that one of them was so high he tried to set himself on fire. I'll admit that neither I nor any one of my companions was ever going to mastermind the scientific breakthrough for terraforming Mars, but we had enough going for us to avoid setting ourselves on fire.

I have had a lifelong habit of always taking along provisions when the availability of food or the presence of any kind of eating facility is up for question, such as at that rock concert—and I do mean a lifelong habit. When I was as young as 10 years old, my seven-year-old sister would often become enraged at our mother for refusing to let her do anything she wanted, and my sister would then dramatically announce that she was leaving home. Every time she did this and headed for the door, I intercepted her and dragged her to the kitchen where I forced a peanut butter sandwich and a container of water onto her. I was not trying to help her go, just go in a prepared manner.

She always screamed that she wasn't hungry or thirsty, and I always patiently and repeatedly explained that I knew she wasn't hungry and thirsty right *then*, but she would be hungry and thirsty *later*, thus trying futilely in my 10-year-old way to emphasize the necessity of taking along supplies to ensure survival. My sister would depart, sometimes with but usually without my food and water, march up our one-lane gravel road about a hundred feet, and resolutely take a seat on the weed-infested bank where she would brood and seethe. My mother always ignored this. The first time it happened I questioned my mother, but she just continued crocheting while saying calmly, "Oh, she'll come back," and of course she did.

After a couple of these dramatic departures, always in broad daylight on warm days, I figured out on my own that my sister would always come back, especially come sundown. I spent too many nights escorting that girl to the bathroom—within the same house—to believe she would stay outside in the dark, surrounded by nothing but a dirt road to nowhere and dense woods haunted by the hair-raising cries of all the unidentified birds and animals that she so skillfully imagined would gulp down a seven-year-old in one satisfying bite.

Fast forward eight years to 1971 when I was 18 and in Colorado. My roommate talked me and the guys we were seeing into accompanying her as chaperones for some kids on a retreat up in the Rocky Mountains. The only instructions we were given was to bring a box meal. My roommate, however, refused to take a box meal because a box meal wasn't "cool." Despite my urging, she kept saying scornfully, "No! We'll just go to McDonald's."

Now . . . we were headed into the Rockies, which are reasonably well known as a vast wilderness where people have perished for lack of food or stayed alive only by eating each other. So I kept urging her to take food, saying, "There isn't going to be a McDonald's within 500 miles of that place."

As it turned out, I was wrong. There wasn't a McDonald's within 800 miles of that place. If you were there without anything to eat, and you still wanted to eat, you were going to have to trap it.

We set off toward those mountains in a caravan of vehicles, loaded with people armed with huge box lunches containing a full two-day supply of food. I had relied on my roommate to advise me about food arrangements. Thus I had understood that after we left the prairie and started climbing to higher altitudes, we would either stop somewhere to eat lunch or fortify ourselves with our box lunch before continuing on. Then at the end of our long trek, we would enjoy a hearty dinner that evening and breakfast the next morning, provided for us at the retreat site. As a result of my misplaced trust in my roommate's grasp of essential details, I had dutifully gathered only enough food for lunch to accommodate myself and the man I was with—a pint container of cherry tomatoes, two pieces of fruit, and six ham-and-cheese sandwiches on hamburger buns. My male friend was quite practical, and he had more than enough sense to bring along food, but he had relied on me to feed both of us because I had told him I would make up the box lunch. Had I known we would never stop for lunch, boxed or bought, and there would be no evening meal or breakfast at the retreat, I would have packed half a grocery store into the backseat of his green GTO.

All other members of our wagon train knew where they were going, but we did not. Thus we couldn't abandon this convoy, not even long enough for a fast-food stop, yet still find them again and make it to our destination. As a result, when we all finally halted beside a lake in some remote mountain valley, not one of the four of us had eaten all day, and when the man I was with noticed that our two companions had no food, he sidled up to me and murmured: "How much food did you bring?" I told him. He did not look happy.

We split my meagre supplies among four adults, two of them possessing the voracious appetites of physically fit men in their mid-twenties. We each ate one thin hamburger-bun sandwich, leaving the other two sandwiches to be stared at because no one wanted to be the uncivilized person who grabbed them. Each of us was privately wondering how to handle the situation, when my friend said to me, "Are you going to eat that sandwich?"

I said, "No, you can have it."

God knows I wanted that sandwich, but he was twice as big physically and at least three times as hungry. My roommate's man looked at her with the same question, and she graciously caved, though I know that had there been no witnesses, she would have wheedled that sandwich out of him. I wanted to throttle her for not listening to me as to how McDonald's builds its restaurants where there are plenty of customers—and not in some obscure corner of the Rockies that saw people the last time some seventeenth century mountain man hiked through on his way to discovering the Pacific Ocean.

Well, a year after that incident, I was in London attending that concert at the Crystal Palace Bowl, and as always, I was the one in the crowd with sense enough to take along some food, though it wasn't much, just some snacks, as we were supposed to be able to buy from vendors. In fairness to my companions, part of my keen alertness to the food issue was a consequence of being the only one present, except for my friend Paul, who was not stoned. Thus I was one of only two people present who still had the ability to remember that there was an insignificant little item called "food" that we might require in the course of an 18-hour day.

We arrived early in the morning and grabbed good seats on the ground up close by the lake's edge, although in a genuine mystery lost to time, my snapshots were taken from much farther back. How we ever got back so far, I really don't know. Perhaps latecomers arrived and crowded in front of us and we kept gradually and courteously scooting back to make room for them.

That morning began clear and bright, but anyone who has spent any time in England knows that it has only four actual weather conditions—misting, drizzling, raining, and raining harder. Our clear bright morning quickly became a misty morning, and English mist is both continual and deviously subtle. The air is just kind of misty in a manner that you don't even realize is getting you wet until you're soaked through. Then you notice that it's no longer misting because it's drizzling, which is okay, you just open your umbrella, which you carry with you constantly, like a sidearm in a war zone. A bit later a thick rain begins restricting visibility, but you trudge on, and it's only when your umbrella is no longer protecting your head, but instead is tilted forward in front of your face and held like a battering ram to cut a path through the raining harder that you cave to nature's supremacy and seek the nearest shelter.

Our nearest shelter was my dainty umbrella, as useful as a handkerchief for shielding seven people. After a time, we didn't try to stay dry. We just sat all day from about eight a.m. until about midnight in the mist, the drizzle, the rain, and the raining harder.

Despite my heavy sweater and long pants, I was cold, soaked-to-the-skin wet, and hungry enough to eat things I did not even like. The wet and cold had intensified the hunger in all of us, but we had no food beyond what little I had and whatever forgotten snacks anyone else was surprised to find in their lint-infested pockets. In that massive crowd, locating whatever vendors existed—if any did, for none lay within our sight—yet still finding our seats on the ground afterwards would have tested the homing skills of even the most sober members of our group. In the space of 16 hours, our meagre supply of food got distributed among the seven of us, plus anyone we did not actually know but who happened to slip in the mud, fall down near us, and gaze at our small bag of chips with yearning eyes.

It rained all day, and at some point the rainstorm augmented itself with some thunder and lightning. It's a wonder we were not all electrocuted while sitting on that wet ground. One well-placed bolt of lightning would have fried the entire crowd. The concert was not supposed to last until midnight, only until late afternoon; but some ambitious promoter had dreamed up the bright idea to film it for later television broadcast, and setting up for the filming plus waiting for breaks between the lightning strikes to avoid electrocuting the performers and crew delayed all the acts.

Joe Cocker was the final act—or at least the last one we saw—but he did not arrive on stage until some moment shy of midnight. I really liked Joe Cocker and I wanted to see his performance, so Paul and I sat all day and half the night on the ground in the mist, the drizzle, the rain, and the raining harder just to see Joe Cocker. Nowadays I would not sit in the rain to see anyone, absolutely no one, but that's because I have smartened up enough since back then to know that certain things I considered doing at age 19 (such as sky diving) and certain things I actually did were at least two-thirds crazy, and in the "actually did" category is sitting all day and half the night in the rain and mud to see the tiny, faraway figure of a stranger, indistinguishable at that dark, rainy distance from any one of the 500,000 people blocking my view.

"Seeing" Joe Cocker is all we did, because minutes after he took the stage, we hastily left to catch the last underground back to our London hotel and its hot shower and clean bed. It was either weakly surrender to that luxury or add another eight hours to the 16 we had already spent wallowing on the ground in our sloppy mixture of cold mud and wet grass.

At somewhere near midnight, we reached familiar streets near our hotel, but we couldn't find a place to eat. I don't know what it's like now, but in 1972, England did not have the "open all night for your convenience" business approach that represents the best of America to Americans who venture abroad. Town shops shut down in late afternoon or early evening. Finding an establishment that sold anything edible after eight o'clock was an achievement worthy of a bold print entry in a memoir, and, in our case, on that particular night, we feared that if we even chanced upon any respectable nightspot that was still open, our drenched, muddy, bedraggled appearance would bar our entry.

Good fortune favored us though, or so we thought, when, nearly hallucinating from 18 hours without food, we finally found a restaurant. Although it was preparing to close, the manager was willing (to our profuse declaration of gratitude) to stay open long enough to serve the last remnants of the only thing they had not yet discarded—spaghetti.

I was never crazy about the taste of beef. I ate it only once in a while and stopped eating it completely after leaving England, but I spent my childhood eating a lot of things out of sheer hunger that I did not exactly want, so downing a bit of beef to satiate my hunger was not beneath me. Or at least it wasn't until I took one bite of what was placed before me. When that spaghetti hit my tongue, every cell in my entire body rose up in refusal just like a stubborn eight-month-old in a highchair that turns its head away when you're trying to spoon food into it. I put down my fork and discreetly emptied the contents of my mouth into a napkin.

I said, "I am not eating this. I don't know what this is, but this is not beef."

Paul said, "Oh, it's beef. It just tastes different because they use canned meat over here."

I said, "This isn't beef. This is a rat they killed in the kitchen."

He said, "No, no."

I said, "Then it's an alley cat they caught out back."

He again shook his head in dismissive refusal to relinquish the blissful pleasure of hot food warming his cold body and finished cleaning his plate while patiently and tolerantly ignoring me, sitting opposite him and repeatedly warning: "You're going to be sorry. That's a rat or an alley cat, and it's going to make you very sick."

I choked down one of the dried out, stale rolls, and we left for our hotel to happily revel in hot showers and the joy of a clean bed. About two hours later, we were both up and in the bathroom. He was there to vomit. I was there to clean it up.

He was so "green" with sickness in every bodily cell that we feared he needed a doctor. I couldn't even say "I told you so." In fact I was *never* able to say, "I told you so." Even after he was well, I could not bring myself to say it, because he vomited until his head hurt, and though we didn't seek a doctor, the aftereffects lingered for about three days.

Although I still say it was a rat, there is a chance Paul was right in saying it was food poisoning from spoiled beef, because a lot of their restaurants in the lower to medium price range were not clean. The sanitation standards (of that time, anyhow, I can't speak for now) were way below what they were in the States. In fact, one restaurant that a friend dragged us to somewhere in London was *filthy*, which was no surprise, because this friend was so tight that he patronized whatever cheap establishment would provide him with a six-course meal for about a buck fifty. He once left a half penny for a waitress at a London restaurant, and she, in her fury, chased him out of the building and screamed at all of us to tell him never to come back. Despite my unwillingness to accompany him to a restaurant of his choice—knowing his lack of good taste in such matters and fearing exactly what we ended up in—he dragged Paul and me to an eating establishment that, according to him, had "the best food in the country."

We were seated by the kitchen, and when the door swung open to release the waitress into our midst, I casually glanced over and into the depths of what had to be the filthiest kitchen on planet Earth. The floor was ankle deep with rotted food scraps that had missed the buckets of slop, scattered strategically around the room. Even the walls were festooned with splashes of dirty water and the fetid residue from garbage. The most incompetently indulgent inspector from any American city's Health Department would have shut this place down with a single glance.

I began gagging and nearly vomited. I refused my food when it came, and the management demanded I pay for it anyhow. Paul was also gagging, but he choked down a portion of his. I could not. (Keep in mind that I had eaten frogs out of a creek when I was a child, so you know a place is dirty when someone who has eaten frogs from a creek can't eat there.)

During the two years that Paul and I lived in England, we consistently had a difficult time finding inexpensive but clean shops to grab a sandwich and a bowl of soup. So we were delighted to finally locate such a place in London, right off Russell Square. It was perfect—soups and sandwiches off a grill behind a counter, and everything out in the open and shining and clean. They had the best creamed chicken soup I have eaten anywhere, and he loved their cheesecake.

Then one late afternoon/early evening, we stopped in on our way back to our hotel after a day gallivanting around London. We were the only people there, just us and the cook, who was bored and leaning against his grill. I was facing him, and I happened to look up to see him idly cleaning his nose with his fingers and wiping it on his apron. I nearly threw up.

I never told Paul what I saw.

The worst thing was—I really hated to think that maybe that's why that chicken soup was so good.

# Chapter 6

# Favorite and Not-So-Favorite Roommates

During the four years I was in the Air Force, I had an astonishing 15 or so different roommates, but I had so many because most did not last longer than a few days. One or the other of us, for one good reason or another, moved out quickly. Two of these women were extremely negative people, and in both cases, we spent no more than one month together before I lit out for more harmonious territory. About three were absolutely wonderful, and the others were mostly compatible except perhaps for some little quirk that made living with them a real challenge.

Among the quirky ones was Katie, a perfectly wonderful girl in all respects except that she came home from work at five p.m. each day and went straight to bed. Because our room was a 12-by-15-foot space, this meant that for me to be active in our room, I had to tiptoe around all evening so as not to interfere in her sleep. I went to bed on the same schedule as most people do who work an eight to five day—sometime between ten p.m. and midnight (usually closer to midnight)—in order to get up at seven a.m. and be at work at eight, which was also the same time Katie had to be at work.

She, however, got up at two a.m., exactly two hours after I went to sleep, which is why, at five o'clock each evening, she collapsed into bed. She made no effort to gradually push her "to bed" schedule forward until it aligned with that of other people—the most important of those other people being me, her roommate—but that was not the only area where she possessed a deficient understanding of the word "consideration."

The moment her blaring alarm woke both of us at two a.m., she snapped on the 100 watt table lamp between our beds plus the ceiling floodlight hovering over our beds, completely oblivious to my inability to return to sleep with 400 watts of light bouncing off my face. Then she banged and slammed closet doors and dresser drawers, trotted off to the shower, and upon returning, fired up a hair blower that roared like an F-15 engine and dried her hair exactly three feet from my ear. This continued for days, while I made increasingly demanding but still polite requests to no avail that she stop lighting up the room and generating all that racket. Then one middle of the night, at the commencement of her usual two a.m. assault on my senses, I, suffering from about a month of sleep deprivation, came roaring out of that bed like an enraged tiger and nearly tore the room apart.

After that, the noise stopped and the lights stayed off.

My first roommate in Colorado Springs in 1971 was a genuinely malevolent person and one of the two roommates I've had who were best left to house themselves for the entirety of their lives (the other being the troublemaking bigot in Omaha), but my second roommate in Colorado was a delightful party girl named Connie, who eventually married and moved out to be replaced by a very compatible roommate, and one I really liked, despite her aversion to box lunches and her delusion that we could easily locate a McDonald's lounging in the depths of the Grand Tetons.

Connie patronized an establishment called the Kit Kat Club, and she kept after me for weeks to accompany her, swearing it was the most fun a girl could ever have. I was seriously suspicious and discreetly checked around, trying to determine what the place was like before I committed, but the only other person I could find who had been there was Marty, my coworker and the girl who eventually replaced Connie as my roommate. This future roommate told me—in the understatement of 1971 and with the same keen awareness she exhibited in regard to the necessity of box lunches: "It's not the poshest place in town, but you might enjoy it."

That place was a dive. Had I been older and more experienced I would have known that the club's name was itself a dead giveaway as to what it was like, for it was a concrete block building situated on the edge of town, boasting a functional décor of sawdust-covered floors to soak up the blood from the bar fights, wobbly chairs and tables made of old, splintered, nailed-together boards—both the weapons used in those fights and their remaining remnants—no windows (glass is a fight hazard), and smoke that hung thick enough to hide the paint peeling off the walls and ceiling.

However, being uninformed of these significant details, I finally agreed to go with Connie just to be friendly, a friendliness I began demonstrating the moment we arrived by sliding into the first seat available just inside the door (I didn't want to penetrate the room too far and lose sight of the exit) then staying rooted to my chair and turning away a stream of men all evening. I had been raised in an environment in which women did not patronize bars, and my inexperience, my 18-year-old youth, and my conditioning were not exactly compatible with that sexually charged atmosphere, filled with about 250 young, single, lusting men, all of whom were shifting around in their pants and praying this would be their lucky night.

So . . . I was sitting there, wishing I had accepted the date with the dorky guy who wanted to sit in a park and watch cars drive up and down the side of Pikes Peak, when a somewhat attractive blonde woman in her early thirties arrived and took the table next to mine. Within a few minutes, a man of about her age approached, sat down, and shortly afterwards they got up and left together. For me, that was like watching one of the country music songs I had heard all my life play out right in front of my eyes. I was rigid with fascination at seeing an honest-to-god Honky Tonk Angel get Picked Up after she had Gone Wrong because a Man Had Cheated On Her, although, looking back on that after a few more years of worldly experience, I realized that with the swiftness of their transaction, she must have been something a little more or less than an angel.

The men kept coming, asking for dances. I kept smiling and shaking my head no, mortified that they thought I too was a Honky Tonk Angel who had been Done Wrong, though the only person who had done me wrong that evening was my roommate who had told me that dive was the hottest place in town and I would have a ball. Finally, the men stopped coming and left me to enjoy the band, for I will say this about the Kit Kat Club. It had the best amateur rock band I have ever heard. That band was a mixture of black and white musicians, rare for that time, and they were extremely good and the only reason I did not phone a cab.

Connie spent every night flirting and dancing and having the most fun a girl could ever have at the Kit Kat Club, and I do mean every night, all night, despite having to get up at seven a.m. to be at work by eight. She routinely stumbled home at four a.m. and plunged into bed to snatch a brief nap before darting off to work all fully refreshed and rested, but when I moved in with her, I was unaware of how her work schedule interfered in her party schedule; therefore, I was completely unaware of how she managed to maintain both.

The first morning I woke in her room, I was physically jerked right off my mattress and onto the floor by a cacophony of sounds like the combined din of two dozen different alarm systems going off simultaneously—which is exactly what it was. Her clock radio shot on at volume 10 screaming the Doors' "Don't You Love Her Madly." Alarm clocks all over the room—on the desk, behind dressers, on the floor, under tables, even in closets—were ringing, beeping, whistling, clanging, clanking, and jangling in a united tangle of painful, penetrating noises. I rolled to my knees on the floor, fought off my blankets, and in a crazed frenzy began lunging at all these different sounds, wheeling and twisting in gymnastic spasms all over the room in a hysterical effort to locate their sources. She had positioned several of these alarms in the most unlikely places (stored in closets, under her bed, hidden in drawers, out of reach up near the ceiling) because their purpose was not just to wake her, but to force her to drag herself vertical and hunt them all down in order to turn them off.

After I had all these machines quieted and my heart rate slowed, I pounced. I landed right on top of her where she still lay all wrapped up and unmoving in her blanket—she had not yet budged, not even to groan or roll—and I began shouting and shaking and tossing her around in her bed trying to get her awake.

She came halfway alive: "Huh? Huh? Huh?"

I kept shaking and shouting, and when she was finally aware of me, I yelled, "Why in God's name do you have all these alarms set?"

She grunted out a groggy, "It's the only way I can get up."

I took a deep breath and got control of my temper—which had been aroused somewhat when I jackknifed out of bed like a semi-truck on an icy highway—while I pondered my certainty that I could not risk jeopardizing my heart every morning. Finally, I said, "Okay. From now on, we will set only my alarm (a quiet little beeping thing), and I will get you up."

We worked it that way for the four months we roomed together, but it was not easy to physically haul her out of her bed every morning, stand her up, then keep shouldering her upright while I shoved her toward her closet and her uniform.

Of all the roommates I had that I liked and enjoyed, one girl from basic training remains my favorite. During basic, I had three different roommates because none of them could withstand the regimented training, and they ended up calling home, pleading and weeping copiously, and some Air Force officer, with admirable detachment and restraint, released them without comment to their irate parents, who were not happy that their little girls were unhappy.

Of these three roommates, the first was an adorable Alabama girl named Carol. The southern girls were a delight to start with. One of our male class instructors gleaned immense pleasure every day from crisply asking one girl from Georgia where she was from, then smiling with great affection for her accent as she obligingly took the next 30 seconds to say: "Geeooorrrrrggggggia."

Carol was not as skilled as the Georgia girls in dragging out a word to its full length, but she could still elongate a syllable. She was the nicest, friendliest, prettiest person, but completely out of her depth in the military. Every night she would lie in her bed, staring at the ceiling in the darkness, sighing; then, dragging out her words in that soft Alabama accent, she would say: "Ooohhhh, if I were hooommme right noowww, I'd be goiiinn-ngg to pahhhhhhhties."

And on the other side of the room, I would groan, "Carol . . . go to sleep. They're going to yank us out of these beds at five o'clock."

On our second day, the training instructors gathered us in the community room to instruct us in how to make a bed and clean our rooms to meet inspection requirements. Carol listened to that in a state of paralyzed panic. When they dismissed us to go perform those tasks, the very moment we were in the privacy of our room, she let loose: "I don't know hooooowwww to make a bedddd. I've never maaadddee a bedddd."

I stared at her, confused, and finally asked: "You've never made a bed?"

"Noooooo."

61

"Well . . . who made your bed at home?"

"The maaiiidd."

I absorbed this before I said, "Ummmm, okay, I will help you. It's real easy. But for now, you take this broom and do the sweeping, and I'll make both beds."

I turned away then turned back, because she had not moved. She was standing, holding the broom at arm's length, as if it were a copperhead she had caught by the neck and the length of its body was dangling toward the floor, and she was staring at it in utter bewilderment.

She asked in the most genuinely perplexed tone: "What do I dooooo with it?"

I said: "You sweep the floor." And to help her out, I gripped an invisible broom by the handle and make a back and forth brushing motion.

She wailed: "I've never sweppptt a floooorrrr. I don't know hooowwww to sweeeppp a flooooorrrr."

I wasted no time in further investigation of who was responsible for Carol's lack of education in basic survival skills. I just went over and took the broom and showed her how to use it.

Carol was no bimbo airhead. She was not stupid. She was simply out of her box. She learned instantly the moment she was told or shown anything, including our physical chores, and had she stayed, she would have discovered that she liked the Air Force. She would have realized that the military is a melting pot of a whole variety of people from different walks of life, different regions, different religions, different economic levels, different educational levels, different life experiences, different ways of thinking—and that it was good for her to experience all these new people with all their new ways.

I tried hard to persuade her to stay. I repeatedly told her that the six weeks of basic training were not the Air Force, that she had already completed one week, now two weeks, with only four more to go, and once those six weeks were behind her, she would even be able to go to all the parties she missed so badly.

But, every night she lay in her cot, under a sheet and a rough wool blanket, staring at that barren ceiling in the darkness, sighing and moaning, "Oh, if I were hooommme right nooww, I'd be having sooo much fuuunnnn. I'd be goiiinnngg to paahhhties . . ."

She called her parents who came and retrieved her, to my regret. I took a snapshot of her before she left because I knew I would never forget her. I still have that 50-year-old picture. She's standing by her bed in our barracks room, wearing her nightgown and smiling so softly. She was the only person I have ever met that I would use the word "sweet" to describe. She was just simply sweet, utterly adorable, and I easily could have gone the entire four years with Alabama Carol as my roommate.

# Chapter 7

# Killing Me with Laughter

**In 1971, when I was 18,** I was living in a girls dormitory in Colorado Springs, and in the room next to mine lived these two black girls.

And yes, I said black, not "African American," partly because I fail to see how anyone who was born and raised in this country is an "African" American, and partly because I refuse to bow to political demands that we segregate the human race according to skin color, and partly because when I was growing up, "Negro" was the preferred, respectful term and "colored" was insulting. Then "Negro" became insulting and "black" was respectful. Then "black" became insulting and "African American" was respectful. Now the wheel has turned right straight back to the original term that had once been so insulting, and I'm supposed to say "people of color" to be respectful.

I know that if I only live long enough, "black" will once again be stylish—after it is re-interpreted to mean "mystery, depth, the infinite, the Divine Soul"—and we'll all have to return to droning on about "soul food" and "soul music," and people will once again start demanding to be called "black" in order to be shown respect.

So, since I've already lived long enough to know where we're headed, then let me begin this story once again by repeating that when I was 18, these two black girls lived in the dormitory room next to me, a white girl. (Okay, if you insist, a Part French, Part Dutch, Part English, Full-Blood Shawnee Paternal Great-Great-Grandfather, and Half-Cherokee Maternal Great-Great-Grandmother American.) Two of their girlfriends, also black, visited their room just about every evening. They had no other friends I ever saw in the 10 months I lived beside them—despite a host of possibilities of all races and ethnicities in that three-story dormitory containing at least 200 girls—because the four of them had only one topic of conversation, and the limited nature of their discourse inhibited the desires of others of any color to associate with them.

Every evening they gathered in their room to repeat the same monotonous statement at the top of their lungs as to how all the white people in the world should be killed. Although these girls came from a big city ghetto, they conversed in a religious call and response manner and interjected praise for each other's repetitions in a bad imitation of the backwoods revival meetings of my youth—"Amen, Sister Angie, you speak the truth," and "That's right, Sister Josephine, I ain't never heard it said better."

I regarded their evening revival meetings with an amused objectivity, because, with my Appalachian background, I fully understood the "he needs killin'" mentality, though I could not help but note with superior disapproval that these girls had not learned to discriminate between killing just for the sake of killing and killing for the sake of need. Their killing urge needed some fine-tuning before it would ever meet the quality standards to which my backwoods upbringing was accustomed.

Before I go further, let me explain that I never got trapped in any of the many social movements of the 1960s and early '70s— race, gender, and so forth—because, by 1968 and age 16, I was already viewing all the morons rioting in the streets and all the campus idiots burning buildings to gratify their craving for violence as the manifestation of a primitive mob mentality, born of mindless emotions. In fact, when I was only a 17-year-old high-school senior in 1970, I did a paper for a political science class in which I said that very thing and further stated that the college kids involved in this "antiestablishment" movement would be living their parents' lifestyles in 20 years and probably be a hundred times greedier and more selfish and materialistic than their parents ever were. My teacher was fresh out of college and not more than about 28, and he vehemently disagreed: "No! No! This is a new world . . ."

Sometimes I wonder if he remembers me.

So, in 1971, although I was only 18, and I was living in Hippie Haven Colorado Springs, my general mindset through which I listened to the moronic "all whites should be killed" routine emanating from the next room was mostly boredom.

These girls would not speak to anyone, but especially not to whites. Every day I passed one of them in the hallway because her schedule was similar to mine, and every day I smiled and said hello, and every day she stared stonily ahead and refused to even acknowledge my presence. Where I grew up, the refusal to acknowledge another person's presence, even that of a total stranger, was just plain bad manners, and though I had to learn, after I entered the big city, to close out men by not acknowledging them in order to prevent sexual approaches, I was not going to allow another female to act like that. I continued to smile and say hello every single time I encountered her and her stony, straight-ahead stare.

Eventually the day came that the girls next door added background music to the revival meeting din that issued from their room. Almost every evening, the moment they arrived home to begin their daily cultivation of useless emotional and mental states (All White People Should Be Killed), they put an LP on their record player at high volume, though I could still hear—above the music and through the wall—their shouted statements about killing all white people. Many of the other girls who lived on that floor complained to each other about their loud music, but no one would tell them to turn it down because no one wanted to get on their list of people to be killed. (All People Who Don't Like Loud Music Should Be Killed)

I, however, took an extreme liking to the female singer and was dying to know who she was so that I could buy the record. She did a gospel-tinged blues version of "Bridge Over Troubled Water" that was pure art. To this day, when I hear that song in my head, I hear her singing it, not the original Simon and Garfunkel version, as nice as it was. Yet I didn't dare go ask who the singer was because, first, I would not get an answer, just a stony stare, and second, they would put me on another hit list. (All White Girls Who Listen to Black Artists Should Be Killed)

I knew the singer was black because no white girl was going to sing like that, but I had never before heard her. In those long-ago years, black artists and white artists were routinely separated when it came to radio play, except for shallow stuff such as the Supremes, who set my teeth on edge, but rhythm and blues artists were not played on "white" stations—and where I had grown up, stations catering to whites were all we had. Fortunately, luck intervened in my favor; it was a live album, recorded at one of her concerts, and one evening, the girls next door set the needle at the very beginning of their record, and I heard the singer introduced to the audience: "Aretha Franklin—Live at the Fillmore West."

I exited my room at lightning speed to find and buy that album, though I never played it while still living there because I heard it from them every day—and too, I thought it might be wise to stay off their list of All People Who Play The Same Music We Play Should Be Killed. On the other hand, had they ever asked me about it, I would have told them flat out that I was one helluva lot closer to her gospel/blues roots than they were as it was the first music I ever heard—on an antique hand-cranked 78 rpm record player. Furthermore, they listened to her only because she was black (had Aretha been white, they never would have listened to her), whereas I listened to her because she could sing, so I had more right to her music than they had.

The weeks wore on and their war councils convened in a relentlessly repetitive evening ritual, completely unvaried in content or volume, all of which I had learned to block out so well that one evening, I had been unconsciously hearing this voracious argument coming through the wall for about an hour before I realized that the content of their session had altered into a real verbal battle. For the first time, they were disagreeing about some of the finer points of their usual four-headed soliloquy. So I tuned in for a few minutes—not hard to do, I didn't have to strain—and crumpled to my bed in helpless laughter, certain I was going to die after they heard me laughing and rushed over to kill me. (All People Who Laugh At Us Should Be Killed)

I laughed so hard, so loud, so unendingly that I was forced to heap the pillow and all the bed covers on top of my face and head just to prevent them from hearing, realizing I was laughing at them, and hurtling next door to kill me. By that time I had so many unforgiveable strikes against me—I was white, I listened to black artists, I smiled and spoke to them in the hallways, and now I was laughing—that I was at the top of their list for getting taken out, and I never would have been able to defend myself because I was helpless from being unable to stop laughing.

The four of them were shouting at each other loud enough to drown Aretha—and it takes some lung power to drown Aretha—because they had been expanding their list of groups of people who should all be killed, and they had expanded it to include "all lesbians." The division in the ranks occurred because two of them argued that black lesbians should be spared, and two of them argued that being black should not spare them.

No argument I have ever heard in my entire lifetime of nearly 71 years has been dumber, more idiotic, more unintelligent than that one—and I have heard some idiotic arguments out of my relatives, out of politicians, and out of Marxist "social activists." I was their general age, only 18 myself, but as young as I was, it was still incomprehensible to me that those young girls would spend their valuable living time deeply and fully and exclusively engaged (mind, heart, and body) in an argument so useless, stupid, and wasteful of mind, emotion, and action. I could do nothing in response but bellow with unending laughter.

I laughed all night. I laugh now if I immerse myself in the memory. I did not bother to knock on their door and point out that the two who argued for killing the black lesbians had the correct argument as far as the rules they had set for who should die. After all, since they were going to kill all whites anyhow, without knowing whether they were lesbians, the only lesbians who would even be available to be killed were black lesbians. I stayed in my room, crushed my pillows and blankets over my head, and kept laughing.

I also continued smiling at and saying hello to the one girl that I consistently passed in the hallway. Then one evening, to my astonishment, she answered. Not much, just a curt, grunted, abrupt "hi," still staring ahead, but it was a small breakthrough.

This went on for a while (my hellos and her one-word, brittle replies) until one day, I was strolling down that hallway, and she was advancing toward me, and I greeted her with my usual smile and hello, and her entire being—her face, body, emotions, and mind—exploded into a huge grin and a cheerful hello. I have never forgotten the sight or the radiation. She was beautiful.

I like to think that out there, somewhere, right now, is a reasonably sane and balanced 70-year-old black woman, who sometimes thinks back to when she was a young and dumb 20-year-old girl and caught up in the mindless emotionalism of the social chaos of her time and place, and I like to think that this woman laughs a little to herself in fond remembrance when she recalls the white girl who lived next door, the one who stubbornly smiled and said hello to her for 10 straight months until she finally answered. I want to believe that if she is alive, she remembers me, not my name—she never knew that, I didn't know hers—but me, the white girl next door who made her forget for the space of one huge radiant minute that she dwelled in a black body.

She never knew that she gave me Aretha Franklin, but I have always known that I made her forget the externals, to forget all the "isms" of racism and classism and elitism that her consciousness practiced, and to see only the essence. To my mind it was one song exchanged for another, and to my mind, it was a fair trade, because no one sings "Bridge Over Troubled Water" like Aretha Franklin.

# Chapter 8
# Major Major Major

People who have never served in the military but who have read Joseph Heller's novel *Catch-22* always innocently assume that the characters in that novel are fictional. They are not. They are true-to-life exaggerations of types, and I know this because I met many of those characters while serving in the United States Air Force.

In the Supply Squadron alone, I knew a smaller, less exaggerated version of Milo Minderbinder; a self-absorbed, complacent Aarfy, always seeking the easy way, bedding whatever woman he ran across and thinking he deserved the freebie; a gung-ho Captain who, until the day he went AWOL, was well on his way to becoming Lieutenant Scheisskopf; and a forlorn Nately in love with a French girl who scornfully rejected him because, as she put it, "He pours wine like a peasant."

I also knew a Hungry Joe with a camera, confident that, although he was nearly blind, he was the equivalent of a professional photographer. I still have photographs he insisted upon taking of Paul and me in which the entire picture is an image of everything around us, plus—just barely visible along one edge—a few fragments of arms and legs, possibly belonging to either Paul or me. At one point during those years, I even heard someone say that my contempt for any authority I did not agree with reminded him of ex-PFC Wintergreen about whom Heller's character Chief Halfoat said (with "undisguised admiration"), "That stinking little punk wise-guy son of a bitch ain't afraid of nobody."

Of all the oblivious, muddleheaded officers I met, the most unforgettable was the Major I happened upon one day who was about as connected with practical reality as Heller's Captain Flume.

I was returning to my office one afternoon, when I came up behind this Major who was standing before our office door, his eyes roving over it in a befuddled searching stare. At my arrival, he turned, locked his gaze onto me for about five stupefied seconds, as if a female Staff Sergeant baffled him as much as that door, then abruptly demanded, "Well? How do I open it?"

I gave myself a couple of seconds to process what he had just told me about himself. Then I carefully raised my right hand, cupped it as if over an invisible doorknob, and rotated it slowly while I said, just as slowly to ensure he understood: "You . . . turn . . . the knob."

He gave me a contemptuous look that asked how I could be fool enough to think THAT would ever work, but he tried it, reared back in surprise when the door opened, and clumped inside. I followed, reflexively thinking that if he were our new commander, I was glad I was being discharged in four weeks.

Among my many favorite scenes in the book, my top favorite is Heller's description of practicing for a Lieutenant Scheisskopf parade by standing around in the boiling heat beside a nearby ambulance until enough people had fainted and been hauled off to call it a day. I actually saw that scene played out to a near perfect word-for-word description when I was selected to march in a parade at Offutt AFB in the 110 degree heat of an Omaha, Nebraska, summer.

The real-life representative of a Heller character who I recall with the most fondness, however, was the Major that we all called Major Major Major. I do not know who originally nicknamed our real-life Major (whose actual name I never knew) by the *Catch-22* moniker. The unfortunate Major was being called that (not to his face) when I arrived on the base, and he was still being called that two years later when I was transferred.

When I first encountered our personal Major Major Major just a few days after my arrival, I, at age 19, had not yet read the book or heard anyone mention our real-life Major's nickname, and being so uninformed, my first sight of the Major was a truly baffling and bizarre experience.

The incident occurred one quiet afternoon while I was crossing the warehouse on my way to the ladies' room on the opposite side from the office where I worked. This gigantic building was a former airplane hangar that had been converted to a warehouse. A narrow strip of offices lined each side of the hangar, and at least 200 or more long rows of tall shelves, holding every engine part, tool, and piece of equipment needed to supply a fleet of fighter jets and their crews, filled the cavernous middle.

I was sauntering down one of those seemingly endless aisles in between two overshadowing rows of shelving when I noticed, at a distance, a Major scurrying toward me with his head bent down toward the floor. I was prepared to greet him when he got close enough, but to my astonishment, he abruptly glanced up, saw me, and in a panicked reaction skittered sideways through a gap in the aisle that opened onto another aisle. I, bewildered but being near a gap myself, stepped to it and stuck my head around to peer at him down the length of that aisle just to see him blanch and hurtle through another gap into a third aisle. I pursued him through my own nearby gap in time to see him bolt frantically from the third aisle into a fourth.

I, curious but in need of the ladies' room, realized I would have to take this man down with a flying side kick if I ever intended to say hello to him, and since I did not need to actually speak to the Major, I let him flee and continued on my way. After returning to my office, I told my male coworkers about this strange, perplexing, and oddly behaved Major that I had encountered during my stroll through the warehouse. They screamed with laughter and gleefully informed me that I had just met Major Major Major.

My coworkers explained the origin of the nickname, and the next day one of the guys brought me his copy of Heller's novel for my fuller understanding. In the book, the character's surname is Major, and when he was born, his father in a burst of creativity, named him Major Major Major. When the character enters the military and is promoted to Major, he becomes Major Major Major Major.

The character of Major Major is a shy, tall, lanky man who desperately wants to be liked, but isn't because he is so socially awkward. Consequently, he avoids human contact in every conceivable way. People are allowed in to see him only if he is not in his office, but if he is in his office, they are not permitted to come in and see him. Anyone who wants to talk with Major Major has

76

to lay in wait for him outside his office and tackle him before he can spot them and get away.

The truly hilarious resemblance between the book's character and our real life Major Major was that not only did they act alike, but they also physically looked alike.

I never had reason to try to speak with Major Major, but about twice a week, one of my coworkers would come in laughing and recounting his effort to corner the Major in the warehouse by chasing him up and down the multiple aisles while the Major dodged and darted and scooted in and out of the many convenient gaps and pretended not to see or hear his pursuers pounding after him and shouting out his name.

No one had anything against Major Major—it was impossible to have something against a man that no one could get close enough to talk with—and no one would have dreamed of being so contemptuous and discourteous as to call him by his nickname to his face. We just enjoyed the hilarity of trying to guess which of the many available escape routes the Major would lunge into if he glimpsed one of us coming.

Then, one day, my coworker Jerry strolled down to the coffee shop, which was in the strip of offices on our side of the building. About five minutes later he came racing back, without his coffee but with his entire body—face, neck, ears, arms, hands, every bit of exposed skin—flaming scarlet with embarrassment. He dashed to his office, sank into his chair, and hid his brilliant red face in his hands while he shook all over with a laughter that he could not stop. After about five minutes of this, he got his embarrassment and his laughter controlled well enough that he was able to speak without gasping and tell us all what had happened.

Jerry had been in the coffee shop when Major Major, so desperate for a cup of coffee that he had risked being seen by someone, had sidled in, simultaneously scanning the room for people to avoid. Before the Major, upon spotting Jerry, could launch himself backwards out the door, Jerry, in a sincere effort to offer genuine friendliness to the horribly shy Major, hastily scrambled over, cut off the Major's avenue of retreat, and unthinkingly and automatically burst out with the name we all used: "Hi Major Major! How are you today?"

It took about a week before Jerry's skin returned to its natural color. Whether the Major had noticed or understood the reference, we never learned, but I learned, from observing Jerry's perfect example of a truly exquisite social error, never to make a habit of referring to anyone by a nickname I never wanted them to know I was using.

# Chapter 9

# Never Hand a Kid Blackmail Information

Back around the year 2000, I posted the following story to an online group that I was part of. I found out later that a woman there stole the story, altered its location from a grocery store to a bank, claimed it happened to her, submitted it to some humor contest, and, no surprise, won.

If in all the years since, any reader of this book has run across that "winning story," trust me, it did not happen to her, it happened to my coworker, and the chance that an identical situation took place in her life with the child saying the exact same thing is absolutely zero.

Here's the original version as it actually happened.

During the 1980s, I worked at an educational center that provided coaching for standardized college admission tests. Our office building was situated right next to a shopping center containing a Big Bear grocery store. One day, my supervisor went over to the grocery store on her lunch hour to pick up a few items. Several minutes later she burst back into the office, reeling with laughter.

She had been in line behind a woman who had a little boy about five years old. The child was throwing tantrums, grabbing at the candy in the boxes in the checkout lane and demanding that his mother buy it for him. She kept telling him no. He kept demanding. She kept saying no. He began yelling, screaming, crying. She kept saying no.

Finally, the child yelled at the top of his lungs: "If you don't get this for me, I'm going to tell Grandma that I saw Daddy's peepee in your mouth."

That woman turned twenty shades of brilliant red, grabbed that kid and her handbag, abandoned her cart and everything she had already placed on the belt, and bolted for the door—probably never to be seen again in any Big Bear store anywhere in the state.

## Chapter 10

# He Needs Killin'

**Many years ago,** an online acquaintance sent me a list of advice on "what to do when in the South" that included these three items:

1. When in the South, get used to hearing, "You ain't from around here, are you?"

2. If you run your car into a ditch, don't panic. Four men in the cab of a four-wheel drive with a 12-pack of beer and a tow chain will be along shortly. Don't try to help them. Just stay out of their way. This is what they live for.

3. Be advised: "He needed killin'" is a valid legal defense here.

I have personal experience with all three, and the second one on the list (roadside assistance for car trouble) has happened to me several times, including twice in the hills of southern Ohio (which is physically in the North, but culturally in the Appalachian foothills) on backroads so obscure that only the three people who know the roads exist ever drive them. Yet *still* someone showed up to offer me assistance.

I grew up in those foothills, way out in the woods in a place where people own guns just in case someone shows up who needs killing, which is why as a kid there, as an ordinary part of your education and survival skills, you learn to handle a rifle or a shotgun by the time you're eight years old. Nowadays, with GPS, it's easy to get directions to places like that, but it used to be that someone had to lead you there, partly to keep you from getting shot, and partly because it required the ability to locate "roads" (dirt trails cutting through the underbrush) that city people would never guess were actual roads.

Appalachians have their own unique approach to life, which is a meritorious combination of helpfulness, a quirky acceptance of eccentricities, guns/killin', and a canny ability to instantly recognize those who don't quite belong with them. Although I left there when I was 16, it stayed in my blood, and as a result, when I was about 23, attending college in Columbus in central Ohio, I often took my little car for long drives on those southern Ohio backroads that, even now, still wind unpaved and mostly undriven through the hills of my childhood. I did it to escape the city, the heat, the noise, and to merge back into the scenery, the cool quiet, the aloneness.

Just so you know, when I use the word "backroads," I'm referring to actual backroads. A lot of misinformed people believe anything less than an eight-lane freeway or anything without a string of big city stoplights is a "backroad." More worldly-wise people believe a semi-tarred country road is a backroad, but roads like that are good roads where I grew up. A backroad is a one-lane, gravel or dirt road, tucked into the hills, where maintenance is done once every few years when the county dispatches a grader to level the ruts produced by the winter snows and rains. For those of you uninformed about road-repair equipment, a grader is a big machine with a big blade—kind of like a snowplow—that levels the road by scraping its ruts flat and digging new drainage ditches along its sides.

One summer day when I was about 23, I had parked my car on one of those backroads beside the site of my birth, and I was sitting there gazing at the brush and the weeds and the trees that had enveloped the space where a house had once stood when I heard a vehicle coming—you can hear for a long ways in areas like that—and soon a cloud of dust appeared and rolled my way. It contained a man in a pickup truck who, upon seeing me, stopped, and keeping his engine running, called out the window: "You having car trouble?"

I said no, I had just stopped to look at the scenery, but thanks for asking. He cast a perplexed glance at the weeds and brush, listened to my voice, looked me up and down, seeing only what a lot of travel and a few years in the city had taken from me, and he said: "You ain't from around here, are you?"

Two out of three.

The only thing left was for him to push back the bill of his cap, stare vacantly around at nothing in particular, and say: "Ahh hell, he needed killin'"—and for me to hack up something, spit it on the ground, and answer: "Yup, he shor did."

The second incident occurred not long after the first one. I had parked my car in the exact same spot and left it there while I ambled down to the creek and across to the old strawberry patch. When I got ready to leave, my car would not start or even make an effort to start. The car was only a year old, and it had given me no warning that it was ever going to spring this dead-silent problem on me at the most inopportune moment. Fortunately, the time was only about five p.m., so I still had a couple of hours before nightfall to obtain help. The question was where to find it. I had lived the first 10 years of my life on that road, and I knew every dwelling on it, including where the houses had once been that had since burned down. Not one house or cabin still stood for about a mile in the direction I had come, and another mile in the opposite direction was equally barren of inhabitants. The condition of the road confirmed that it had been a minimum of six months since the grader had been through, which meant I could be there a long time before anyone happened by.

My sole recourse was to pray: "Oh, God, oh please God, let this be the year that the county has enough money to send the grader out twice, and let this be the day they scrape this road"— although I knew I would have a better chance of holding the only winning ticket for the 500 billion dollar SuperDuperPowerBall Lottery for which I had not yet bought a ticket.

After calling on the Lord's help, I considered my two options: set out walking, as late as it was, or spend the night in the car and begin walking the next morning. I had enough food and water to survive comfortably for about five days, 10 if I rationed it, because I always take along provisions on even short trips—a thermos of water for five-minute jaunts and an additional container of food for any journey close to an hour. For a round-trip excursion to a city on the other side of the state (the entire route paved with restaurants, grocery stores, huge malls, and a million inhabitants), well, trekkers through the Himalayas take along fewer provisions than what I take.

For whatever reason, a calmness and expectancy descended after I decided to just sit there and wait for Divine Intervention. About 15 minutes later, I heard a vehicle coming, and soon a battered car, generating the usual cloud of dust, clanked up beside me and skidded to a halt. The driver was a man who was maybe 25, just slightly older than I was at that time. He was accompanied by a withdrawn young woman who turned out to be his wife, and a chattering older woman who was his mother.

After the preliminaries of "You having car trouble?" and "You ain't from around here are you?" the man peered under the hood of my car with an experienced and expectant air before announcing pleasantly that he had no idea what the problem was.

(Later on, after this incident was behind me, my brother Dale told me that the car had left the factory with its starter operating intermittently, sometimes connecting and sometimes not. He solved the problem permanently by adjusting the starter.)

The young man offered to drive me to their home, which I accepted because the offer came with the promise of a telephone and the chance to call a brother who lived in a local town. (Around there, a "local town" was on the other side of another 20 miles of hilly roads that the county's grader visited every few years.) So, I climbed into the car with this trio, never suspecting that my rescuers were going to move our relationship into the third item on the advisory list—the "he needed killin'" as a valid legal defense.

We clattered and banged and churned up dust for about two miles back down the road I had already travelled and pulled in at their place where I made the call. I got no answer, and since this event occurred in the mid-1970s before recorders (or cell phones) were universal, I could not leave a message. I no longer recall how many times I tried to telephone, thus I no longer recall the details of how I got stuck in their home for an extended period of time. What I do recall, and so vividly that it blanked out all less important memories, is that the mother, who had not stopped talking since her son's car had idled to a stop beside me, opened a discussion on the family's plans to kill her husband, because, according to her, he "needs killin'"—an exact quote—and the time she preferred to go through with it, which was later that same evening, just three or four hours away.

Now, I had never seen that woman before in my entire life; so I didn't know if she were drunk and having delirium tremens, crazy and rambling nonsense, or just being herself.

Interspersed with her murder plans were her additional plans for me to stick around as a mate for her son, which I interpreted as a credible piece of evidence that she was severely disappointed in his choice of a wife and thought he could do better if he opted for me. From the looks of his poor withdrawn wife, she was equally certain that she could have done a bit better herself in the acquisition of a mother-in-law, and I was betting that if the killing ever started, that girl would spring out of her coma and take out the mother with the first blow.

I was quickly realizing that I had met a sufficient number of the family to acquire enough information to make a competent decision that I did not need to extend my visit in order to meet the intended murder victim. Maybe he was the only sane one in the bunch, or maybe he was so crazy himself that he had driven the woman crazy. I didn't know. I did know that I stood a far better chance of getting out of there while the odds were only three against one than if I waited around until a fourth staggered through the door, possibly waving a sawed-off, 12-gauge shotgun in one hand and a half-empty whiskey bottle in the other.

I also clearly remember wondering whether the mother was speaking freely in front of a stranger because she did not intend to leave any witnesses who could testify against her—and I remember this because that uneasy thought was the one that motivated me to engage in a vigorous effort to distract her from any such concerns by pretending I had neither heard nor understood her murder plans. The years have faded my memory of the details of my responses and all my various convoluted actions and reactions that I used to convey my lack of comprehension. All I recall is cultivating a blank expression, which I desperately hoped was convincingly oblivious to any and all her plans in regard to both the murder and the vitally important need to dispose of the body by burying it up in the woods and telling anyone who asked that the old guy was out hunting. If I vanished too, as one of the few people who ever passed her way, her story would last her lifetime and beyond.

By the way, I am not exaggerating this incident. I'm toning it down because, when it happened, I jotted into my daily diary only these essentials that I'm relating here, and because it happened so long ago, I don't recall all the additional details of events and subtleties of conversation exchanges that made it far more complicated than this brief summary.

I do recall, vividly and with great sympathy for the son, that he was absolutely mortified. He was acutely embarrassed by both his mother's murder plans and the sexual suggestions for me. That guy was wishing the earth would open and swallow him, and of course he knew he wasn't going to luck into that just when he needed it. When he abruptly leaped to his feet—insisting my car would start, it had probably just flooded, and he would drive me back immediately—his need to escape the crippling embarrassment his mother was causing him was the comforting reason why I did not hesitate to climb back into his car and be alone with him along two miles of narrow dirt road through solid woods as nightfall rapidly approached.

Had he not been so consummately humiliated, I would have feared he had inherited his mother's inclinations, and I would have run those two miles. Had he come after me, he would have discovered, when I whirled around and made a stand, that he should have consulted someone other than his mother for romantic advice.

The moment we were safely sheltered from his mother inside his car, he said, almost bitterly: "I'll bet you're wishing we had never come along."

More precisely, I had been thinking, "Why in hell didn't I wait another year for that grader?" But all I said was: "Oh, don't worry about it, I've seen worse," which was true. I had. After all, he hadn't met some of my relatives.

I didn't go into specifics, however. I did not want him learning we had anything in common and start thinking that maybe his mother had a brilliant idea about the two of us sharing an intimate domestic future. Even a temporary relationship was not in the cards, let alone a marriage. He was actually a nice man, a decent man. He was not bad-looking either, and he had a natural, intuitive attunement to me. I really was thankful that he had happened along and tried to help me, and I was bursting with endless gratitude that he had the brains and sensitivity to realize his mother was an embarrassment and he should get me away from her and back to my car. But, just in case his chromosomes included his mother's deficiencies, with the danger of them spurting into manifestation at any moment, I maintained a mental and physical state of red alert while riding back alone with him.

By that time, we were well into early evening with nightfall closing fast, and oh lordy, I was praying my car would start. Nighttime in the woods is a *lot* darker than nighttime in the city, and I did not want to be there after dark. Having spent the first 10 years of my life living on that road, I was not afraid of the woods or the darkness, but if I were going to sleep in my car—even with it locked and part of my tire jack in my hand, which is what I would be holding and where I would be, because there was no way in hell I was returning to their house—I preferred to do so without anyone knowing I was there. If someone accidentally found me, they found me, but I did not want anyone to come looking for me at about two a.m. As it stood, far too many people with killing on their minds already knew my whereabouts.

When my car started, I was so obviously relieved that he commented on what a relief that must be to me. I thanked him and pulled away as if I were in no hurry, meaning, I was careful not to floor it, and I didn't yell out the window, "Hey, thanks. Tell your mom I hope her plans work out."

In the end I think the mother must have slept off her drunk because I kept a lookout in the news for a few days, and I didn't hear of any murders taking place in that neck of the woods, which doesn't mean it didn't happen. A body buried back in those hills was never going to surface, and if she covered it up by saying, "The sonuvabitch just up and left me," anyone who knew her would say, "Yep. Saw that coming."

# Chapter 11

# Ole Spike and the Schoolmarm

During my mid-twenties, I worked in the state of Ohio's Bureau of Employment Services. Anyone who has worked a job that deals with the public knows that a large percentage of the "masses" are unusually crazy and therefore responsible for many bizarre, hilarious, and sometimes dangerous incidences. We enjoyed our share of noteworthy encounters, although most of them were a consequence of our office building's location being in an area of Columbus that was, well, let's just say it was not near a prison, but it should have been.

It was the kind of area where certain expectations were routinely met as mine were one evening when I left work and discovered my three-year-old car would not start. One of my male coworkers kindly offered to search under the hood for a possible cause and found it without any real effort when he noticed my battery was missing.

Our building was in a strip shopping center, sandwiched in between a bank on one side and a Kroger grocery store on the other, and either the bank or the Kroger store frequently got robbed, an excitement I found somewhat startling during my first few weeks of employment. In time, however, I accustomed myself and became as skilled at ducking for cover as my fellow workers, which we had to do, because the robbers' escape route was always in through our building's front door on a zigzag course in between and around all our desks and cubicles, over the scrambling arms and legs of frantic, wild-eyed workers, and out through the employee exit at the rear. This eventually drove Marsha, the supervisor of our unit, a tall, elegant woman who looked like an African Queen, to shoot to her feet every time the sirens blasted, and scream, "Bolt the doors!"

At some point, the State hired a new employee for our office without investigating him well enough to learn that office work was only his sideline. His real calling was increasing the membership of a church he had started somewhere in town by "witnessing for Christ" to all the dispirited people who dragged their anxiety riddled selves into our office to sign up for unemployment benefits. The unemployed, and especially the newly unemployed, do not have a lot of patience for anything other than the offer of another job and a generous check to cover their bills and feed their kids. Since they were already enraged, depressed, and frightened about the downfall in their financial affairs—and therefore in no mood to hear about all the material wealth waiting for them in some gold-plated heaven, following their earthly demise when they would no longer need the money anyhow—they complained vehemently, and an angry, embarrassed management counseled the preacher man to cease and desist.

Under this threat of an abrupt change for the worse in his own financial affairs via an immediate relocation to a new position within the line of unhappy people on the opposite side of that unemployment counter, the preacher managed to restrain himself until the day Ohio's governor of that time, James Rhodes, arrived in our office, accompanied by a stiff group of officious political figures and a strutting horde of self-important media personnel, to perform a ribbon-cutting ceremony that included Rhodes giving a speech. These 50 or so guests gathered in our huge lobby where a small dais had been erected for the governor, and we 50 or so employees all took seats facing the governor and his personal band of political and media groupies.

The governor began talking—about what I have zero recollection, because just as he got roaring, an "Amen" rang out in the lobby. The governor went dead silent. Everyone did. The only sound was the whooshing hiss of close to a hundred heads whipping around in search of the source. Everyone who worked there knew exactly who had brought down the Lord's blessing on the governor, and furious, embarrassed expressions settled on the faces of all employees except for Art, Carol, Mary, and me. The four of us did not bother to search for the preacher man in the crowd. We searched for each other, unanimous in our shared sense of humor and knowing exactly who else would be making a locked-jaw effort to restrain the laughter that would tumble us off our chairs.

The governor was an old, experienced politician, but even with his lifetime of coping with unexpected interruptions, he still needed about eight seconds of silence to gather his bearings before he could resume his speech. When the second "Amen" rang out, followed by, "That's telling it, Brother Rhodes," he momentarily halted, then plunged right on without pausing again—or even blinking—to the continued and repeated revival meeting shouts.

I never heard a word of that speech. I sat hunched over, staring at the floor, my legs crossed, my teeth and lips pressed together in order to clamp my jaw closed. The merciful second the governor finished, I leaped to my feet and ran to the restroom at the rear of the office, the only place in the building with enough privacy to conceal sound. I never made it inside that toilet, however, for just outside its door, I collided with my three coworkers, who were also running hard to the same privacy, and our combined atomic bomb of laughter exploded in that hallway.

The four of us always considered the same situations that upset our coworkers to be hilarious, and one of those was a prank my coworker Art pulled on me.

To understand this, you need to know that I have never had the slightest interest in becoming a schoolteacher. The very thought bored me. Yet the aura of "the teacher" has haunted me since I was a small child. People would say to me, "Oh, you're going to grow up to be a teacher," and I would answer, "No, I'm going to be a basketball player or a painter." (I wavered between sports and art.)

When I was a college student during my twenties, people never asked my major. They just always said, "Oh, I've heard their teaching program is pretty good," or "What's their teaching program like?" Sometimes they assumed I was in the nursing program, but mostly they chose the teaching/education program.

I also constantly heard that I "looked like a teacher," which nearly gave me a complex in my younger days as I preferred to think of myself as a little more exciting than a schoolmarm. At times in various jobs I worked, I was forced to train people in their duties, and I was always told that I was an excellent teacher. During my early thirties I worked in the administrative area of an educational center, and people often assumed I taught there. Even palmists got into the act. When I was 22, a palmist told me that I had the Ring of Solomon, denoting great wisdom, combined with a square, signifying a master teacher. In short, this teacher corona surrounded me throughout all my life and in all my circumstances, and one day at the Bureau it enveloped me.

We had this biker who came in every so often to speak with a claims officer about his unemployment claim. He was quite large, not fat, just a really big guy. He took a bath probably once every few months or so, and his long stringy hair saw soap and water about as much as the rest of him did. I'm not sure how often he brushed his teeth, although it wasn't important because the street fights had eliminated his need for dental care. He always wore the usual biker garb, leather and chains, little throwing knives, along with two metal, spiked wristbands for ensuring victory in close encounters. I never really knew what all he had hanging off him in terms of shiny, metal weaponry, because the big overhead lights that blanketed our ceiling glared off everything down below, and when the lights caught him, I lost track of what I was seeing.

At any rate, every time he came in, he dealt with Art who was about eight years older than I was and afflicted with a wild sense of humor that was his most redeeming trait. Art kept a can of air freshener in his desk to use after Spike's visits because a certain stinky odor lingered, and it was Art who began referring to our biker friend as "Ole Spike" in honor of the wristbands. It was also Art who first noticed that for some reason, Ole Spike treated me like a queen, and Art phrased it that way, "Watch this, he treats her like a queen."

None of us could figure out why Spike did this, because he and I were the most unlikely pairing in all of existence. All I could assume was that I had nothing against the man, he had never done anything to me, and all that weaponry he wore did not scare me, so I was nice to him. I looked him in the eyes, smiled, and courteously acknowledged his presence as my mother had taught me to do with all people, and he was nice in return. I can say to you with full honesty that Ole Spike was a true gentleman toward me. I never would have been afraid to be alone with Spike, because Spike would never have compromised me, and I sincerely would have trusted him to put his life on the line to protect my maidenhood, if I had still had it by the time I met him.

Art regarded Spike's reaction to me as being hysterically comical, and he never passed up an opportunity to tease me about it. Sometimes the jokes got a bit off-color, as when I came to work after spraining an ankle from slipping on wet grass on a slope, and Art warned me that in the future I should advise Spike to remove his hardware.

But most of Art's jokes revolved around this dress I wore. My financial situation was rather restricted in those days; thus my ability to buy clothes was rather restricted. It's not that I was on a limited budget; it's that I did not have enough money to even set a budget. I constantly had to find creative ways to buy clothing by using change only and without employing actual dollars.

As a result, I was in a shopping center one day, flipping through the clearance rack in a Sears, when I ran across a dress that was so ugly and so unsalable that it had been marked down from about fifty dollars (high for 1979) to three dollars. Even this was costly, but I thought maybe I should spring for it. The problem was that the dress was hideous, a nondescript saggy red rag that drooped off the hanger. So I flipped past it and flipped past it, but I kept returning to that three dollar price tag until I finally decided it couldn't hurt to try it on.

I was stunned to discover that I didn't look half bad in that dress. It was a plain, dull, long-sleeved, knee-length, tomato-red, knit shift, with a "shirttail" hem (a very short, curved slit on each side like a shirttail). The dress had a high, very slight V-neck. I decided that with chocolate-brown shoes and a matching brown leather belt, both of which I already had, to take up some of the droop, the dress would look okay. So I bought it.

That dress turned my life into a nightmare. For some reason, men went nuts. Every time I wore that dress—and I wore it only about 10 times over the three years that I had it—total strangers would approach me with dinner invitations or with marriage proposals that went like this: "Would you like to get married for about two weeks?" Or " . . . married for this weekend?"

These encounters with strangers became a major problem because our office building was in a shopping center where there was ongoing, bustling activity. After my car battery was stolen, I began parking in the mall's public lot in front of our building (instead of in the more concealed and private rear employee lot) to ensure that anyone tampering with my car could be seen; however, my new parking space forced me to walk across the lot between my car and our building's front door, which I could not do—if I were wearing that red dress—without getting stopped and offered dinner dates and marriage proposals. I have no idea why because the dress was not overtly sexy. It fully covered me right down to my knees and wrists. The high V-neck showed no cleavage, and it couldn't have anyhow because I had none to show. At five feet, five inches tall, and 120 pounds, I did not have a voluptuous figure. Eventually the dress ended up hanging in my closet (because I couldn't take the hassle of wearing it) until I cut it up for rags and used it to wax the car.

The first time I ever wore that dress to work, Spike came into the office to talk to Art. That was also the first time I personally encountered Spike, and Spike reacted by treating me like a queen. When Art started teasing me about this, he concluded: "It must be that red dress."

About six weeks later—with my clothes closet being as limited as my budget—I was out of things to wear that did not repeat what I had worn the day before, and in desperation, I risked the red dress again, thinking maybe the first reaction to it from men had been a fluke. When I arrived at work, Art had a field day, saying, "Oh, I see you have your red dress on. Spike must be coming in to see you." He kept this up all morning in variations; then, that afternoon, in sheer coincidence, Spike ambled through the door, flashing hardware in all directions. When Art and I set eyes on Spike, we laughed until the tears ran.

Over the next eight months, every single time Spike strolled in there, I was wearing that red dress. Yet I wore it randomly and infrequently, and Spike's visits to our office were just as random and infrequent. To Art and me, this repeating coincidence was hilarious. (Just so you know, I actually have an affectionate memory of Spike, who must have thought the red dress was the only one I owned. He was the last man I would have taken up with romantically, but that doesn't change the fact that I almost liked the guy.)

Then, one day, I was standing in my supervisor's office, and I have never forgotten what I was wearing because it was so conservative—a knee-length, pleated black skirt, low-heeled, plain black pumps, a high, round-necked, plain black sweater, under a blazer that had red and black checks on a white background. I have worn glasses since age nine, and I have never worn makeup. The only non-conservative thing about me was my chestnut hair, which was halfway down my back.

Art suddenly came running into the office, hunched over with contained laughter, barely able to speak and get out his words, saying: "Oh I have just played the worst joke on you."

I was instantly wary and asked, "What did you do?" because Art often took his jokes too far.

He asked if I had noticed the man he had been dealing with—a nice-looking, nice-acting man of about 30, dressed in a conservative business suit. I said yes I had seen him, why? In between hunched-up gasps, Art managed to blurt out his story.

The businessman had seen me across the office and asked Art to introduce us. Art had given him a polite but firm no, saying he did not do that kind of thing, and if the man wanted to meet me he would have to introduce himself. So the man began asking Art questions as to what my interests were and if I had a boyfriend. Art confirmed that I had a boyfriend. (I had just met Doug, so I did, although Art did not know this nor did anyone else in the office as I always kept my love affairs as secret as possible.) The businessman asked Art if the relationship was serious.

Art said, "I don't know how serious it is. It seems pretty serious. He comes in here often."

The man then asked "what his competition was like," and Art gave that man a detailed and vivid description of Ole Spike.

I said warily, "You didn't."

Art, gasping laughter, said: "I did! I did! I swear to you I did, and you know what he said?"

Apparently, the businessman stared at me across the room for a long time before he said slowly, "I never would have believed it. She looks like a schoolteacher or a nun." Then he just shook his head in full acceptance of my biker girlfriend status, leaned in to Art and confided, "You know, you just never know about people. You can't tell anything about them by looking at them."

Art and I laughed until our throats went raw. We hung off each other, the furniture, the walls. Some of my female coworkers were outraged, thinking they were looking out for my best interests, as in—what if I had wanted to meet the businessman? How could Art tell someone such an awful thing about me and ruin a potentially great romance?

And it *was* bad. That was the crazy part. It was *so* bad. It was a terrible lie to tell about me, yet I couldn't get angry because it was also so *funny*.

(I wasn't interested in that businessman to start with, but I would not have been anyhow, for he had been able to tell a great deal about me by just looking, yet he did not follow his instincts. Any man I would have wanted would never have gone against his own instincts.)

That incident took place when I was 26 years old, just shy of 45 years ago as of this writing. Even now, sitting here, remembering it and writing it down, I can't keep the huge grin off my face, and it's because I knew back then what was going to happen.

Right now, somewhere out there—if he's still alive—is an elderly businessman, and every time he sees a motorcycle or a biker or someone mentions either one, he gives a shake of his head and says in a tone of sober disbelief, "You know, one time when I was about 30, I was in this office, and I saw this girl, real conservative looking girl, you would have bet anything that she was a schoolteacher on her days off . . ."

Then he proceeds to tell the story of the schoolmarm who gave her heart to Ole Spike.

# Chapter 12

# For the Love of Sports

Basketball was the first sport I played. I was only six years old when my older brother Dale showed me how to toss a basketball from down in between my legs, up into the air, and through a metal hoop nailed to a tree. When I was 10 years old and in the fifth grade, he came home from the Army, caught me still shooting the ball that way, and said no little sister of his should still be playing sissy basketball. By the time his Army leave was over, he had me dribbling, doing hook shots, jump shots, and learning how to foul out. At that same age, I fell in love with baseball and began living just to play it during every school recess—a devoted daily practice that transformed my adolescent self into a good pitcher and a home-run hitter.

At age 18, a female friend in Colorado introduced me to tennis, which she detested playing with me until after I had learned to modify my home-run-hitting baseball swing to more of a baseball line-drive swing. A few years later I acquired an agreeable partner for tennis in Doug, although we did experience a bit of unpleasantness one warm afternoon when I, dangerously unaware that he could be touchy on the issue of his athletic skills, casually mentioned that he was playing like a girl. Within seconds I was dodging tennis balls that came whizzing across that net with alarming speed and intentional targeting.

Doug had golfed during his teens, and he kept insisting I would be a natural at a game that I had concluded from meticulous observation had obviously and deliberately been designed to bore participants as well as observers. Critics of baseball grouch about its slowness, but at least baseball contains random spurts of lively moments that require you to run as fast as you can.

I assured Doug that compared to golf, I probably had more fun as a kid in contests with my brother Randy to see which of us could hit a distant tree with a rock, but Doug persisted and eventually persuaded me to accompany him to a driving range where I, clad as Doug was in old khakis, tennis shoes, and a clean T-shirt, reclined on the grass and watched respectfully while he whacked a bucket of balls into a field. He had brought along a shorter club that he conspicuously dropped on the ground right alongside my outstretched legs with, as he explained afterwards, a sneaky hope that if I stared at it long enough, I might feel motivated to pick it up.

I could have comfortably ignored that club for eternity. What brought me to my feet was the arrival of three robust men, somewhere around age 30, who took up commanding positions next to me, all the while exchanging brisk, authoritative statements about drives and handicaps, strutting smartly in newly purchased, straight-from-Vogue golfing outfits, and swinging impressively expensive clubs, which they removed with manifest confidence from the depths of real leather, monogrammed bags. But if that golf ball had been a volleyball, they couldn't have hit it.

I passed an enjoyable several minutes watching them swing like Hall of Fame hitters and send clumps of sod soaring at each other while their balls rolled limply off the tees and stumbled to a stop just a few inches from their official golf shoes. I knew I could not possibly embarrass myself any worse than that. So, I picked up my club and swung and discovered I could do worse because I completely missed both the ball and the sod. However, now that I was on my feet and active, Doug eagerly jumped forward to coach me in the details of how to stand, where to place my feet relative to the ball, how far back to swing the club, and other professional advice that I did not fully register and therefore did not fully heed. I tried again and the ball hooked off about 50 feet to my left. My next swing clipped the top of the ball, spurring it into a rabbit hop of about two feet.

Finally, on the fourth swing, I asked Doug to step back, reasoning that since it hadn't mattered so far how I swung or where I stood, and since I was never going to take up golfing anyhow, therefore professional stances and guidelines were irrelevant to my golf swing, I should give my body the freedom to enjoy itself by doing whatever it wanted.

That drive flew straight and true all the way up and out to the 250-yard marker.

Doug exulted: "I told you! I told you that you'd be good at this!"

I modestly said it was pure luck, but I swung again and put the next one in the same spot. With nothing more to prove, I returned to my seat on the grass and resumed entertaining myself by smiling in friendly fondness at those three muscled men as they dug up sod and smacked six buckets of balls into each other's shins.

My approach to golf will not surprise anyone who understands 1950s or 1960s rural areas and small towns. In that environment and in those decades, we learned early to let our bodies choose how to play a sport while we ignored all professional guidelines, along with, for the most part, actual rules, for I clearly recall that we never played a game according to the rules. First, rarely did anyone even know the official rules, and second, we had only one real rule anyhow: All rules would be adjusted to suit any condition.

In other words, if nine people completed a team, but we could round up only five, we took the five and didn't quibble about irrelevances such as numbers—or skill, sex, size, and knowledge of the game, which was often recognizable anyhow only by the kind of ball we were using. In our baseball games we did not permit sliding at second and third bases, though only a fool slides when second base is a telephone pole and third base is a rose bush. Fly balls intercepted by the telephone pole were automatically foul—an essential rule that prevented a batter from getting an easy home run while the opposing team scrambled to figure out which direction the ball had bounced. And, of course, we adhered to that universal and ironclad rule applicable to all baseball played in rural areas: Anything hit into the weed-covered field beyond the fence was an automatic out. Otherwise we had to call the game off for an hour while we searched for the ball in the brush and the honeysuckle.

We played basketball with similar flexibility. We made allowances for the way our outdoor "court" sloped. We never forced a player to dribble on the rocky places because it flipped the ball sideways and out of control. Any player backed into the ditch was given a chance to climb out, but he or she wasn't allowed to shoot while everyone's guards were down. If someone shot anyhow, the cheat shot didn't count, and the ball was turned over to the other team.

I happily progressed through the first 16 years of my life playing sports in this manner, oblivious to any other possible approach. Then, at age 16, I moved and landed in the junior class of Marietta High School, a school with a large enough student body to create two actual basketball teams during a single gym class, which was indescribably exciting until I learned that these two teams were shackled to a hideous blight that I had never before heard of called "girls" basketball. No amount of the adaptability to the unexpected that makes up my nature prepared me for the rigid, rule-infested atrocity of "girls" basketball, which the fortunate young females of today are naively unaware ever scarred the lives of their mothers and grandmothers.

Our physical education teacher was a woman with the meanest face I have ever seen on a human being. She was close to six feet tall and rail skinny—not slender, skinny. Slender promises shape. I was slender; she was skinny. She had close-cropped, iron-grey hair and a nasty, squinched, mean face, the likes of which I have seen on only one other creature, a scrawny, starved and vicious feral cat that used to live in our nearby woods. I will say flat out—ignoring all appalled demands for "political correctness"—that if that woman had ever been laid in her entire life, and I doubt she ever was, it was by a desperate man or woman who had not been laid for the same length of time and had run out of options. An air of malevolent frustration lingered around her, and she took it out on the girls who fell under her power in her physical education class.

When I mentioned her to my older sister-in-law who had attended that high school, she said, "Oh my god! Is that old biddy still there? All of us girls hated her, and we were terrified of her."

Nothing had changed. Gym class was a tense ordeal of silent, frightened cowering on the part of nearly every girl present.

I had attended the school for less than a week when I strolled happily into my first gym class, which, up until then, had always been one of my favorite classes, and that awful woman selected me from a lineup of about a hundred girls and ordered me to climb up on a balance beam, saying she was going to grade me on all the apparatuses, and I was to start there and perform various jumps, somersaults, and splits.

Now, I had never before seen a balance beam, let alone did I have the ability to perform on what is possibly the single most dangerous piece of equipment in women's gymnastics. When those tiny Olympic-skilled girls climb up on that thing and start bouncing and flipping and launching themselves in multiple directions, my muscles tighten just to watch them, and those little girls are the world's best.

I did not immediately realize the woman was talking to me because I had never before had a gym teacher afflicted with such an unsurpassable lack of brains in regard to the safety of her charges. So, I just stood there, ignoring her and searching the crowd to see which unfortunate girl was supposed to climb up on that thing, until she harshly reissued her demand while glaring my way, and I finally understood that this idiotic order was directed at me.

Before I go further, I must mention that I cannot say her selection of me was based in any desire to "pick on the new kid," because this school was large enough that even most of the students knew only a few of their fellow classmates. I was just another body in a crowd of thousands, unnoticed by either classmates or teachers, none of whom could have told you whether I had been in that school for one day or one decade. This woman chose me because she was a malicious and partially insane sadist. Backflips and forward somersaults on a balance beam are gymnastic maneuvers requiring careful and extensive training, *lots* of careful, extensive training. You don't pick some kid from a crowd of strangers and order her to do those.

I reacted with the only sane response possible. I said a firm: "No. I will not."

She kept ordering. I kept shaking my head and saying a quiet, "No."

I offered no explanation for my refusal as I did not realize I needed to. I was operating under the delusion that this woman was only two-thirds stupid, not completely stupid; thus she could reason out by herself that since I could not do a backflip on a floor the size of a basketball court, surrounded by acres of flatness to save me in case I missed my footing, there was an excellent chance I also could not do one on a four-inch wide board that was four feet off the floor.

She threatened to fail me. (Let's see now, do I opt to become a quadriplegic, or do I choose to get a failing grade from an Old Biddy, yet I'll still be able to walk in and pick up my report card?)

When I continued to refuse, she snarled for half a minute then directed me onto a balance beam that was about seven inches off the floor. That was a height I could confidently hop onto and unerringly walk along its full length, but when I again calmly and steadfastly refused to even attempt somersaults and back-flips, the Old Biddy snarled some more and ordered me onto the trampoline.

I gladly obeyed that command. I had not been on a trampoline for three years, but I had loved it, and I was naturally athletic enough that I knew my body would instantly recall and perform the basic knee, seat, and back drops—although that unintelligent woman never should have ordered a total stranger onto a trampoline either without first questioning as to whether I had ever before seen one. She simply got lucky that I had, and lucky too that I resisted the temptation to deliberately bounce off onto the tile floor and kill myself in order to send her to the State Penitentiary where I thought she belonged. In her relentless determination to scale the heights of colossal ignorance and jump from there into the bottomless depths of downright stupidity, she again began demanding double and triple somersaults and other complex trampoline maneuvers from me. Once again I calmly refused, until, in a final act of deep frustration, she abandoned her effort to coerce me into committing suicide-by-gym-equipment and told me to get off the trampoline.

A few days later, I arrived in her class to discover basketball was on that day's menu. I was thrilled and even more so when the Old Biddy immediately put me in the game. My thrill vanished within five minutes when she abruptly halted the game and left me standing on one side of the court in isolated bewilderment while my teammates crowded together on the other side and cast baleful, long-distance glares at me for causing them to lose the game. Pacing in between us was the Old Biddy, screeching rules, threats, and penalties.

I was to play *girls* basketball she screeched. I was not to dribble as that was for *boys* basketball, and I was, she observed insightfully, a girl. My only role was to bounce the ball three times and pass. I absolutely was not allowed to shoot. (Uhhhh . . . I could sink a basketball from the center line of our high-school court as long as I was standing still and could set up for it. What idiot would deny me the chance to shoot?) I was never to cross the center line, never scramble, never go for a rebound, never steal, and never sweat. My role, she screeched repeatedly, was to stand like a bored android waiting for someone to bounce it three times and pass it to me so that I could bounce it three times and pass it to another droid. My only other role was to confine myself to one side of the court and do absolutely nothing except stand there in clunky, flat-footed limbo—with drooping, drooling jaw and boredom-glazed eyes—and observe what little action was taking place down at the other end as the two forwards and the center from my team tried to prevent all five members of the opposing team from doing anything that resembled actual basketball.

Calling that atrocious, moronic, idiotic mess "basketball" was sheer blasphemy.

The Old Biddy ended her tirade by screeching that I would be thrown from the game if I committed one more "error," and a minute later she carried out her threat. When she asked why I was sitting cross-legged on the floor during the middle of a basketball game, I told her that I was hoping someone might roll the ball my way. She choked and gurgled and, to my relief, threw me out. She didn't ask why I did it, but had she asked, I would have told her: You adapt the rules to fit the conditions of the game.

# Chapter 13

# Peaceful Wilderness Living

Camping is something I can do if necessary, meaning, if I have no other choice, but it's not an activity I seek. My younger sister Jean adroitly summed up my reason after she was coaxed into some camping trip: "I grew up like this. I just didn't know it was called camping."

When her husband of that time, while discussing her childhood, said he would "like to live that way for about a week," she told him, "Uh huh, about a week is all you could take it."

When I was about 25, back in the 1970s, my older sister Sharon dragged me on my first weekend camping trip by extolling the appeal of "peaceful wilderness living" and "getting away from it all." (The "all" being the entire array of attractive and useful accouterments of civilization—electricity, refrigeration, air conditioning, comfortable beds, indoor bathrooms with showers, flush toilets, and hot and cold running water.) Sleeping out in the rain and using the toilet in the woods assisted by a handful of leaves was too reminiscent of my childhood for me to regard it as anything except an unfortunate return to what I had escaped. Nonetheless, I trudged along with her, her husband, and their (at that time) 15-year-old daughter Tanja, buoyed by the promise that I would be sleeping inside a camper, which sounded as grand as a five-star hotel when up against my other option of sleeping inside a thin bag on the cold hard ground.

That night, peaceful wilderness living gave me a nightmare. Tanja had wisely grabbed the narrow top bunk in the camper, leaving Sharon and me to bed down together in the bottom bunk, a much wider space because both the bunk and its mattress conveniently folded out. Sometime during the night, that two-part mattress separated, forcing my body to sag in between the mattress's two halves and inspiring me to dream that something had seized me around the waist and was dragging me downward into some bottomless pit. In a marvel of precision timing, Sharon chose that exact moment to crawl over me to visit the toilet. Just as she had her body squished inside the two-foot space between the top bunk where Tanja was sleeping and me, on the bottom bunk where I was dreaming, I unexpectedly screeched in her face. Sharon panicked, and because she was already on top of me and occupying all the minimal space between the two bunks, when she clenched my shoulders and commenced shrieking "What is it? What is it?" directly into my face, she did so from a point that was only about three inches from my nose.

I came half awake to find my nightmare had materialized as an actual physical form. A huge, powerful, shadowy, shrieking hulk had me pinned to the bed. So I launched an immediate offensive attack by upping the volume on my screeching and hurling my entire body against hers in a frenzy of self-defense. Our heads had just enough space between them to give us both the necessary breathing room to continue shrieking at each other's noses as I tried to heave her onto the floor and she thrashed violently in several directions in her inability to hold me still. I managed to smash her upward into the bottom of the bunk straight above us, which she hit with a magnificent thumping jolt that woke Tanja. Tanja yelled something indistinguishable above the din Sharon and I were making, which brought my brother-in-law in the opposite bunk just far enough awake to groan, "Whaa-a-a?" and kick the wall as he rolled over, thereby creating, within the camper's tinny interior, a resonating sonic-level boom that I interpreted as my monster's friends jumping through the wall to help put an end to me.

Well . . . we eventually got that small misunderstanding straightened out, but after that, a second camping trip with Sharon was not in my plans. I just happened to arrive for a visit at the same time someone yelled, "Load this beer in there and we're ready to go," and I found myself in a caravan of vehicles heading for the bushes.

Camping, as I learned on that trip, is a wonderful opportunity to acquire valuable survival skills, such as what we are willing to eat and drink when compelled by circumstances, because the cuisine on these trips was unlike anything you've ever eaten, mostly because, half the time, you didn't know what you were eating. I've witnessed six or seven people standing around a bean pot trying to identify its contents.

"What's this black stuff floating in these beans?"

"Just bits of ashes. Some bugs. Nothing to worry about."

"That looks like pieces of bark."

"Maybe the kids threw something in it."

I have been served—and I have eaten—fried potatoes so grey with smoke and dust that I thought they were campfire ashes. I almost poured water on them to ensure they were out for the night. Being a non-pop, non-beer drinker, I begged for water and was told: "There's a whole river right by your elbow."

Camping is also educational. I learned the nuances of casting a fishing line as a consequence of spending a half hour watching Tanja's stubborn attempt to throw her line into the river, which was probably easy to do under most circumstances. She, however, had to put it through a four-foot square open space between two overhanging trees, clear the waist-high weeds, skirt the bushes covering the bank, and, if she were real lucky, get the hook to plop into the water beyond an old log jutting into the river with a five-foot spread of flood debris clogged around it. She kept catching it in the trees. Then she would jerk it loose and flip it behind her into a wobbly swirling arc that just barely missed the lawn chair where I was sitting, clenching the chair arms for the support I needed to hunch down each time that hook spun past my head. Finally, I offered to cast it for her.

"You know how to cast?"

"No. I've never done it before in my life."

I did very well for my first try. I did not catch it in the trees; I caught it in the bushes right beneath them. On my second try, I did even better by clearing the open space and snagging it in the log. It took me four tries to get that line where she wanted it—back in the trees. I handed her the rod and reel and moved my chair out of range.

Although casting was not my innate skill, rowing a boat came so easily and instantly that I was the first woman in the camp to master it, which was an exalted moment until one of the men learned how much I enjoyed it and decided I could take him water skiing. I gave it my best effort and he tried to help by shouting, "Faster! You have to row faster," but it's a good thing Carl could swim, because his head was the only part of him that ever got above water.

That second trip was the one during which Sharon suggested I sleep in the tent instead of the camper to get the feel of "real camping." So, I reluctantly made for a tent that had been erected on some of the roughest, most rutted, tree-root-infested ground that has ever materialized in the state of Ohio. I got as far as just inside that tent's entry when I succumbed to a fit of magnanimity and generously offered to decline my pleasure and let someone else enjoy real camping. But Sharon insisted, and by then some wiser souls had snapped up all the available camper beds. According to Sharon, the tent was fine for sleeping because it had foam pads, and I would never notice all those ruts and old tree roots that I kept stumbling over as a result of feeling them right through the tent's floor and my thick-soled hiking boots. Nonetheless, in a spirit of camaraderie, sometime after my eyes had adjusted to peering through swarms of insects, I agreed that the tent seemed hospitable. It was large and the pads appeared to be the substantial barrier that Sharon promised. She slapped us a path through the mosquitoes and said not to worry about them. They'd disappear when the lights went off. I chose not to challenge her, although I had never in my life met a mosquito that was afraid of the dark.

We settled down for the night, and I discovered that the ground on my side of the sleeping mat sloped away from me; therefore, to keep most of my body on the mat—and avoid rolling off and downhill to the other side of the tent—I had to maneuver my body into an L-shape, stick both feet out from under the covers, and lodge them against some lumpy protrusion under the tent floor. Then teenage Tanja appeared and announced that she had no place to sleep other than with us. Tanja wedged herself in between Sharon and me on a sleeping mat that was designed to hold only two people if placed on flat ground, and only one person if placed on sloping ground, but not three people on any ground conditions.

I stoically braced my knees and forearms against the tent floor and the granite-like ground underneath it and managed to maintain a sliver of comfort for my hips and back while I resigned myself to a night of "real camping," which I knew could not possibly get worse. But it did, because somewhere around two a.m. I woke, assuming that one of us had wet the bed before realizing that it was pouring rain, and somehow the rain had invaded the tent, and my sliver of comfort had vanished into the soggy cold depth of a waterlogged sleeping pad.

At dawn, the moment I floated out of that tent and hours before anyone else was awake enough to beat me to it, I shouted dibs on a camper bed for the coming night, but even that preventive measure did not allow me to avoid another rewarding experience of peaceful wilderness living. That day progressed without real consequence into a mild and pleasant evening, and sometime before midnight, Sharon and I were sitting by the campfire with our cold drinks in hand. The other campers were in bed. The night enclosed us in a private cocoon as we sat talking quietly, sharing our thoughts, listening to the river flow. I had barely nodded my head in blissful admission that I finally understood what camping was all about when a horrendous crashing vibrated the woods beyond our small clearing and something dragged itself through the shrubbery. This being the Ohio Valley and the foothills of the Appalachians, where Bigfoot sightings are often reported, not to mention the infamous Mothman and various cryptids of frightening size, appearance, and conduct, I moved nothing except my eyes into a stealthy sideways glance at Sharon.

"Do you, uh, know what that was?" I asked, trying to sound offhand.

"No."

"An animal?"

"Probably."

"Big one?"

"Sounds like it."

A small tree fell and the ground shuddered. Something was confident enough that it felt no need to be discreet, and it wasn't a deer. Although deer are large animals, they are also quiet animals. If you are out in the woods, a tiny chipmunk—and especially a rambunctious squirrel—will make a hundred times more noise than a deer, because chipmunks and squirrels scurry through fallen leaves and twigs, rattling and clattering and rustling up a storm of noise as they go, whereas deer pick up and plant their feet when they walk. A deer can arrive right beside you, and you don't know it's there until it snorts to gain your attention or, if it's a doe, rears up to beat you to death with her front feet because you have accidentally stumbled upon one of her babies that she had hid in a patch of weeds.

I yawned and stretched.

"Would you prefer to go to bed?" Sharon asked.

"Yeah, I should. It's been a long day."

We ambled across the clearing and managed to get about 20 feet from the camper before we broke into a jump-start run. When Sharon, who was in front of me, couldn't stop and slammed against the camper door, I smashed into her, and we both slid sideways, grappling for the handle and elbowing each other in a manic effort to get the door open and be the first one through. As the far more experienced camper in escaping the nameless threats hidden in the dark depths of the peaceful wilderness, she stumbled inside ahead of me and fell over a tackle box in the darkness. I staggered in and jerked the door shut behind me.

"How do I lock this thing?" I panted. "I can't see the catch."

Sharon groaned from somewhere near my ankles. "We left the flashlight by the fire."

"Well I'm not going back for it," I yelled.

"What is *wrong* with you two?" my brother-in-law growled from the corner bunk.

We turned on him. "It's a bear. It's Bigfoot. Tearing up trees. Chasing us."

"Ah, it was just a deer or a raccoon. You should be ashamed scaring those animals."

He went back to sleep. Sharon and I huffed off to sit by the window and watch for Bigfoot. Bigfoot didn't show. Eventually we got bored and went to bed too. But before I fell asleep, I heard her whisper cautiously, "I guess after tonight, you won't be camping with us anymore."

I gave it some thought before I turned my head toward her to ensure she would hear my whisper: "If I ever do, the next time something comes at us from the brush, I'm beating you to the camper."

After that incident, camping lost whatever slim charm it had ever had for me, and I was certain I would never again voluntarily inflict a camping trip onto myself. Yet the first driving vacation that Doug and I took together, back in 1980, was a vacation in which we alternated camping for one night and staying in a motel the next as we drove through the southern states—Kentucky, Tennessee, Georgia, Florida—before circling up through the Carolinas and into Virginia and West Virginia and back to Ohio.

Most of the campsites were hospitable, but there was one unforgettable moss draped, insect-infested campground somewhere in southern Georgia, containing a lake and a sign that said, "Beware Alligators."

When I notified Doug of the sign, he scoffed, "Oh, they just put that sign up to scare kids away from the lake. There are no alligators here."

"There are also no campers here besides us," I pointed out.

"It's early yet. They haven't stopped for the night."

"It's so dark I was lucky to see this sign."

"It's late in the season. No one camps in September."

"All the other sites were full. That's why we're here."

He turned to the clerk. "Two adults, one tent."

"One adult. I'm sleeping in the car."

My fear of alligator teeth shredding our thin tent did not come to fruition, but my fear of how little a tent could protect me against some wild animal, maddened by hunger, rabies, or some equally bothersome affliction, reemerged up in Virginia when we stayed the night at a campground in the Blue Ridge area. This time the sign warned against bears.

Again Doug scoffed. "There are no bears here. They put that sign up to scare . . ."

"Yeah, well, there were alligators."

"I'll bet they haven't seen a bear in years. The sign is a precaution. Besides, we'll be in a tent," he said, dragging out the flimsy barricade that he trusted with a badly misplaced faith.

We had arrived in the early evening, and only two campsites remained, giving us a choice between pitching our home-sweet-home tent near the bathroom on stony ground or pitching it far from the bathroom on soft ground. The choice of a campsite was a serious decision because I'm one of those people who has to use the toilet about every 30 minutes, and while we were debating which site to select, the ranger came along and laconically told us that a bear had been sighted in the vicinity, stealing cookies.

"It was a day ago," he said. "Came right into camp. Those people beside you left out cookies." He wagged his head reproachfully. "Shouldn't do that. That bear stole those cookies right off the top of their camper. He sure was a big one."

As the ranger departed, I repeated, just in case Doug had missed—or maybe dismissed—the ranger's most significant bit of news: "A bear big enough to lift cookies off a camper roof. We pitch near the toilets."

"We don't have any cookies. We have nothing to worry about. Besides, it would be kind of fun if one came into camp. Think of the excitement."

I thought about it and said I'd sleep in the car. He said I had nothing to fear. No bear would tangle with me. I wanted to know just what that remark implied. He said it was time we set up camp.

We resumed our debate on which site to choose, and I again insisted on the stony ground near the toilets, justifying my choice with my usual after midnight run to the toilet and the possibility of wrestling an ill-tempered bear on the way. Doug wanted the soft ground farther away. I reminded him of the bear. He again pointed out that we didn't have any cookies. I said the bear would not know that until after he had interrogated us, which swung the vote for the stony ground. The way I figured it, the closer I was to that toilet, the faster I could get inside the building before any bears started hitting me up for cookies and getting ticked off because I didn't have any.

Doug caved to my choice, a choice that turned out to be a very *big* mistake, for that was one of the most miserable and sleepless nights I have ever spent. Sometime around midnight, the wind picked up, and I lay wide awake and saucer-eyed in my fevered certainty that every tree limb scraping and scratching was that bear, and the only thing preventing my certain death was the thin material of a pup tent. About halfway through the night, the air mattress I was sleeping on to obtain extra cushioning against the stony ground popped its cork, and my body settled against what must have been the hardest stone ever created. Although I knew I was miserable and lying on rock, I genuinely did not realize the obvious—that the air mattress itself had deflated—because my entire being, mind, body and soul, was fully occupied with the task of tuning my ears to every indistinct sound, straining my eyes to see through tent walls, and transforming every shadow that fell across that tent into a bear.

By the time morning rolled around, my pelvis was purple with bruises from being crushed against rock all night. I was in so much pain that I almost would have invited that bear inside to be a cushion I could curl up against. Even more demoralizing was the blinding realization—which nearly knocked me senseless—that we should have gone ahead and camped on the soft ground and saved my body, because I would have urinated in my shoes before I ever would have left that tent. It's not that I thought that staying inside the tent would protect me. I definitely did not. I just thought it would be advantageous to stay out of the bear's sight and not draw any unnecessary attention.

Despite the bruises and the bears, air never tasted so sweet and clean as it did in those Virginia mountains. I have loved the mountains since the age of 18 when I first set eyes on the Rockies, for like the purity of the desert, which cannot be described and must be experienced, mountains too have an eternal nature that cannot be described and has to be experienced.

# Chapter 14

# The Dating Game

I have gone on exactly seven dates in my life, if dating is defined as "accepting an invitation from a man with the intention of getting to know him in order to determine if he is suitable for a long-term relationship." All seven occurred within the space of the approximate one-year period from just a few days before my eighteenth birthday to just after my nineteenth birthday, after which I quite sensibly gave it up as a waste of time.

During my teens, I did not date at all for two main reasons. First, my teen years were so chaotic that I was never in a position to "be a teenager" and socialize in ordinary teenage ways, and second, I was never, ever, *ever* attracted to teenage boys, even when I was a teenager. So I turned away the ones who approached me, even the nice ones, being, probably, the only girl in America who turned down two different high school football heroes (one for a regular date, and one for a prom). Instead, I spent my childhood and teen years patiently waiting to turn 18 so that I could have what did attract me—adult males.

As a result, my dating debut occurred during the summer after I had graduated from high school in June of 1970, when I was still 17, but before I turned 18 that following October, and unfortunately, that first date was thrust upon me by someone else, because the man was not and never would have been my choice.

**Date #1:** That August, although I had been accepted into the Air Force, and I had already undergone the physical examination, which included a pelvic exam, I could not enter basic training until I was legally 18. While I was waiting for my October birthday, my brother-in-law framed me for this date by telling the man, an extremely shy ex-Marine about 23 years old (so I guess I was still what they call "jail bait" and shouldn't have been with him anyhow) that I was interested in him, even though I had zero interest in this man, and I mean *zero* interest. He was not and never would have been a man who attracted me. However, when he called, he was so shy that his voice was noticeably trembling, even over the telephone. I felt sorry for him, and out of sheer kindness and because he had been told I would say yes, I said yes, unable to say no and humiliate him, which was both the first and last time I ever accepted a date with a man out of kindness.

We went to a John Wayne movie, an ex-Marine's standard choice at the time, came home, and exchanged polite goodbyes during which he asked for a second date. Once again I said yes simply because I did not know how to extract myself from the situation in a kind manner. Technically, I went on two separate dates with him, but I count them as one blended experience because the first rolled straight into the second as a consequence of my inability to halt the flow.

The second date was a Barbra Streisand movie, my choice, though what it was about I really cannot say, because I was preoccupied with my certainty that this guy was going to try to kiss me at the door when we got home, and since there was no way I was going to let that happen, I spent those two movie hours busily plotting my escape. The evening ended, we reached the front door, and I, placing my back to him, opened the door, hastily stepped inside, turned, and keeping an arm's length distance between us, graciously thanked him for a lovely evening—and that was the exact and unforgettable moment that my younger sister Jean, who was 14 going on 15, suddenly and to my eternal gratitude, brought all dates with this man to a permanent end.

She and my oldest sister Retha were in the dining room behind the living room, pitting tubs of fruit in preparation for freezing it. Although they were able to hear the front door open and hear me talking, they were unable to see either of us; therefore, they were unaware that he was still standing just outside a wide-open door.

When they heard the door swing open, Jean, without waiting to hear it close, hollered, "Heeeyyyyy Amy! Did he give you a pelvic exam?"

Then she and Retha exploded in gales of loud, belly-wrenching laughter.

His face twisted with fury, and though I desperately wanted to laugh, I managed to keep a mostly straight face until I got that door shut. He whipped around to leave, and I knew even before I heard his car rev and rip out of the drive and scream down the highway in a haze of smoking rubber tires that he was going to do that. I knew he was that immature and insecure. Any man I would have wanted would have laughed and possibly called back some smart-ass reply such as, "I tried, but she wouldn't let me."

Still, I felt I had to defend him at least a little. I marched back to my sisters and said, "Jean!!! He heard you!!!"

She looked up in wide-eyed innocence and said, "Oh! He did?"

"Yes!"

She and Retha took a moment to absorb this by looking questioningly at each other. Then they exploded into another storm of laughter, and so help me, I joined them.

**Date #2:** About five months later, I was in technical school in Denver when I went on a double date with a friend of the man my roommate was seeing. This friend was a sophisticated, good-looking, slick ignoramus from one of the Carolinas who informed me that he was going to marry me and take me back to whichever Carolina he issued from.

He happened to be standing nearby when a palmist in the recreation center read my palm and advised me that I would marry within the next few months. This prediction sent him into a bouncy state of joyous ecstasy, for he actually thought he was that man and his fantasy of living with me in a domestic Carolina paradise was only weeks away from coming true. Neither he nor the palmist would believe me when I told both of them that this predicted marriage was never going to happen, that I would have an affair during the next six months, but I would not marry the man (which is exactly what happened).

Mr. Carolina was undeterred by my emphatic rejection, and when he made the mistake of trying to wrestle me to the car's back seat during that double date in order to slobber in my mouth—while insisting I was "just playing hard to get"—I exploded in a verbal attack that took him apart. He got off lucky, because I was a far more physical person than he ever suspected, and my next explosion would have been physical.

**Date #3:** During those two months I was in Denver, all the girls except me were nuts about an exceptionally good-looking Lieutenant that we often saw around. He would walk in a room, and all the girls would lean toward each other, saying, "Oh my god! There he is, there he is!"

One day, I was sitting in a café with three other girls, all of us in civilian clothes, when he spotted me, came across the room, and asked for my phone number. I gave him the number, despite having no particular attraction to him. I was still young enough and new enough at the dating game that I thought maybe this "getting to know a man" was an effort I should be making. After all, other girls thought the dating of random men was exciting. So maybe my approach of not wanting to socialize with men who did not instantly attract me was going about the dating game all wrong.

The girls seated with me were floored by the Lieutenant's unexpected approach, and the moment he left, they pounced, asking: "How did you *do* that?" I had no idea. He had come up to me; however, his unexpected arrival was a pattern with men that quickly became routine. The men came to me. I never had to flirt or seek them, and in time, with more experience, I just as quickly began to rely on that pattern to select the men who were right for me, while saying no to the others with a smile to avoid being hurtful.

I spent the evening talking with the Lieutenant in the base's recreation center, a quiet building with reading, game, and music rooms that offered an alternate place to go for those of us who detested bars. Sometime around midnight, he asked if I wanted to "go downtown." I said yes, because a large city has a different atmosphere at night and a different kind of beauty. I anticipated admiring the Christmas lights that were still up or visiting some Denver lounge that had a band. I was just barely 18, and like everyone else my age, I was young enough to think that staying out half the night somehow benefitted me. The idea of going home at midnight was not yet integrated into my mental processes.

He called a taxi and a short time later, we pulled up in front of a very large, multi-storied downtown hotel, which I assumed contained some lounge we were going to. As my date paid the fare, I noticed the taxi driver giving me a look, which much later on, after acquiring more knowledge of such things, I was able to describe accurately as a "knowing look," but at that time, in my inexperience, I simply regarded it as an odd facial distortion that I could not interpret.

We entered a tomb-quiet, totally-empty-of-people, gigantic lobby, so big that huge support columns were scattered throughout. All the columns were of a diameter big enough to hide a full-grown person, which I know as a fact, because, while I was innocently gazing around trying to locate the entry to the lounge, and wondering why I could not hear music, he approached the desk and began renting a room, and I, in shocked embarrassment, bolted toward the nearest of those columns, jumped behind it, and began gesturing wildly and emphatically at him to get his butt over to me so that I could privately convey that I could not sleep with him.

This incident wins the top prize among all misunderstandings I have ever experienced. He had assumed that I had understood that "to go downtown" was a polite euphemism for "to go have sex," but I had taken him literally. Had he added a few essential details to his request, such as—and I'm just choosing randomly off the top of my head—"hotel," "renting a room," "removing clothes," and "engaging in sexual intercourse," I would have understood.

By that time, it was about one in the morning, and exhaustion had set in because the adrenaline needed to stay alert for most of the night had shut down after we crashed headfirst up against this solid wall of miscommunication.

Fortunately—and possibly because I would not come out from behind that column—he believed my frantic about-face, and for whatever reason, and though it took some persuasion, I believed him when he said, "Look, we're both very tired. I'll go ahead and rent the room and you can have the bed. I'll sleep in a chair or on the floor. I won't bother you."

He did not. I actually spent the night with him, safely, in that hotel room. However, that first date was also our last date, though it had the benefit of being an early and much-needed lesson in how Lieutenants preyed on young, naïve, enlisted girls.

Almost four years later, in 1974, just a few weeks before I was discharged, a good-looking, charming, red-haired Lieutenant from Oklahoma spotted me in a café, this time sitting by myself eating a grilled ham and cheese, french fries, and a chocolate shake. He came over, courteously asked if he could sit down, then asked me out. I smiled and said no, automatically remembering a similar situation that I had not handled with the wisdom I now had from four years of experience. He was intelligent, college educated, very well-mannered, and hilarious. As he continued to sit there and talk, making me laugh, I was getting ready to ask him if I could change my mind, thinking that he might be a fun guy to spend some time with before I was discharged, when he suddenly said that he had thought I would go out with him just because he was an officer.

I smiled and shook my head. His remark was innocent, merely a natural assumption, because far too many women do choose men based on their rank, their jobs, their cars, their looks, their clothes, their money, prestige or power, their family's wealth and social standing—women even marry men for those reasons and routinely end up divorced or living in misery—but it wasn't worth finding out, when he pulled up to a hotel in downtown Omaha, that his reason for asking me out was his assumption that I would also sleep with him just because he was a commissioned officer.

**Date #4:** About a month after that disaster in Denver in the winter of 1971, I was in Colorado Springs, and my female coworker, who later became my roommate (the same roommate who scorned box lunches and thought I might enjoy the Kit Kat Club), asked me to go to a party as the blind date of a friend of the Army man she was seeing. She assured me that I would really like him because he was extremely good-looking. Although I was just barely 18, I already knew that good looks were never what attracted me to a man, so I dismissed his looks before I even met him. Then after I met him, I dismissed him. Physically he was extremely good-looking, but mentally he was the most spineless, mushy noodle of a man I have ever run across. I intensely disliked him the moment I stepped out of my dormitory and saw him, at a distance, sitting in the back seat of the car—and the feeling was mutual. Why he disliked me on sight I do not know and did not care enough to find out. He did not have enough intelligence for me to value his opinion, and his constant quoting of his former college professors to justify his drug use (we all should "try everything") was the moronic argument of a genuine idiot who was incapable of even one independent thought.

After a 10-minute ride, we arrived at the party in a state of shared dislike so evident that as soon as we were inside the apartment, he searched for an available girl, found one oozing with the same mushy ignorance and weakness that had eaten whatever remnant of a brain he may have been born with, and sidled up to her, leaving me alone. I was glad. Her outstanding feature was that she resembled the actress Eileen Brennan, both in her physical looks and in that seedy, slovenly quality that Ms. Brennan conveyed so well in the movie *The Sting*. I easily pictured this girl at age 45, three times divorced and slouched on some shabby barstool, trying to get some dingy man to pick her up.

I was desperate to leave, but I was trapped. The people I had ridden with had not informed me in advance that they intended to stay the night, and I had not brought along any "mad money" for a taxi home. The marijuana smoke was dense enough to give me a splitting headache, although sitting for most of the evening on the outside balcony in the icy winter air gave me some relief from that. I returned when they all started "crashing"—passing out or falling asleep on beds, chairs, and the floor. I stretched out on a couch. Ms. Seedy Noodle bedded down on the nearby floor, and when someone offered Mr. Mushy Noodle a bed elsewhere he said, "Oh, I think I'll just crash right here," which happened to be right beside Ms. Seedy Noodle.

About 15 minutes after all the lights had snapped out, while I lay nursing my horrendous headache and wishing to God I had never trusted my coworker's judgment in men, the atmosphere transformed, and I realized that the two Noodles on the floor had mushed together like two giant slugs in the most nauseating of ways. I could not hear them—they were being considerate about the noise—I felt them via the way in which the atmosphere was oozing and mushing all around me. Fortunately, he wasn't skilled enough to stay at it for long, or else that limp, wet noodle he had for a spine extended to the rest of him, and they soon oozed apart and slumbered.

I too was somehow able to sleep. Departure time that next morning was a godsend.

**Interlude:** Shortly after that disastrous date, I met my first lover. He was never a "date," because I did not go out with him to "get to know him." I knew him before I even met him, and I confirmed our suitability for each other with my first glance at him. After a six-month affair, he left for Thailand, and a month or so later, I went on my fifth date.

**Date #5:** This man was also an Army guy. I went out with him partly because I was experimenting with dating, and partly because he had a motorcycle, and I liked motorcycles. (My first lover had owned a motorcycle.) I discontinued seeing him after he, while showing off, wrecked his motorcycle with me on it by driving too fast on a dirt road that the bike was not designed for—and that was after I had repeatedly and violently shouted into his ear from my seat behind him that he was going too fast and to slow down.

When that motorcycle went into its slide and while it was still speeding forward, I somehow managed to leap from it to keep it from falling on and breaking my leg. I still don't know how I got off it—and landed on my feet too. All I can say is that when the bike went down, he was the only one on it, and I was already walking away, back to town, so pissed at his juvenile immaturity that I thought I might kill him if I stayed within sight of him.

**Date #6:** I arrived in England in January of 1972, and went on a date with an extremely nice Jewish guy from New York City who wanted to be an actor. He asked me out because I was the only person he had met in the Air Force who knew who Julie Budd was (a young girl singer in the late 1960s who looked and sounded like Barbra Streisand). He was very proud that Julie was from his neighborhood. I accepted his offer to spend the day in London because I had not yet been to London, and I assumed he would show me the sights. Instead, his idea of a great time was to spend all day sitting inside London cinemas watching the latest movies. The girl from the Appalachian foothills and the Jew from New York City had absolutely nothing in common. He paid for a nice dinner; then we took the train home that late afternoon, smiled at each other, and parted company. He was the best of my seven dates, and the only one I recall with genuine fondness.

**Date #7:** I would not remember the guy who was my second date in England—the one who ended forever my attempt to play the dating game—had it not been for how I had to be nearly restrained by a straitjacket to keep from knocking him out of a movie theatre chair, kicking him into the aisle, then pounding him right straight down through the floor. I have no recall of his name, how I met him, where he worked, what movie we were watching, or anything at all about him except for that one minute of sitting in the theatre beside him and knowing that if he did not let go of me, I was going to beat him to a pulp.

Back in the 1950s and 1960s, when cartoonists wanted to show a young couple in love, they would draw two heads pressed ear to ear, usually seated in a movie theatre eating popcorn, with little hearts shooting out from their heads. This guy had seen way too many of those little cartoons.

We sat down in our seats, and while I was absorbed in comfortably arranging myself, he suddenly reached one hand around my head, clamped it over my ear, and yanked my head sideways on my shoulders, forcing my cheek up against his as he leaned toward me, which is quite possibly the most painfully awkward position you can put your head in while sitting upright unless you can rotate it 180 degrees, bend it backward onto your chest, and hold it there for 16 hours. With his free hand, he grabbed my arm, jerked it out of my lap, up and over the chair arm, and trapped it between the chair arm and his body. Then, using his free hand, he began lightly fingering the center of my palm, thinking (I assume) that this was going to arouse me sexually.

The only thing he aroused in me was a violent, physical desire to knock him off me and hammer him into the floorboards.

I cannot tolerate tickling my own palm, let alone can I tolerate some man doing it. Any man who wants to handle any portion of my body had better have a firm touch. I managed to restrain the physical and verbal violence, surging through every cell of my body, long enough to break loose from this idiot without breaking every bone in his body, but I knew right then that he was the end of the line. I was never again going on another date just to "go out" and "socialize." I was never again going to waste my time on men that I knew with one glance I was not and would never be interested in for any type of long-term relationship.

**Interlude:** About a week later, I met my second love and spent the next two years with him. He too was not a "date." I did not go out with him to "get to know him to see if I wanted to marry him." I knew from the first moment that I would never marry him, but I also knew he was the right man for a wonderful, long-term affair.

**Finale:** So, just three months after my nineteenth birthday, and after only one brief year of exploration that yielded seven disastrous dates of one degree or another, I withdrew from the dating game. I have never regretted that.

The simple fact was, I was not like other girls. I did not need to "get to know" a man via dates, because I never needed more than a few minutes in a man's presence (and sometimes a mere glance sufficed) to determine whether we were suited for a long-term relationship. This meant that I turned away some very nice, very attractive, very suitable men—for someone else. Since I always knew which ones were or were not long-term for me, to "date" the ones who were not, just because they were nice or attractive, was wasting my time and theirs.

Even worse, it was lying to the men. For me to accept a date with a man was to imply that we were embarking on a joint effort to determine our suitability for a longer or more permanent relationship, but when I already knew which men fit that, to date a man just to "go out" was to lie to him, to mislead him into thinking we could be something more permanent.

Right about the same time that I gave up dating, a girl in my dorm was preparing one evening to go out to dinner. She had obviously spent a great deal of time on her appearance and choice of a beautiful lace dress in order to look as elegant as possible. I complimented her, and because we had the same general circle of friends and coworkers, I also asked who was taking her to dinner. When she told me, I was so stunned that all I could do was repeat his name with about 15 invisible question marks hanging in the air after it. Although we were all friendly with this particular man—we tolerated his lack of character and always accepted his company—he was not a person who was attractive in any manner at all, and I knew that was how she regarded him.

She returned my paralyzed stare, genuinely and sincerely astonished that I did not understand, and in a tone that implied her reason should be obvious to anyone who was not a complete moron, she said: "Well . . . it's a free meal."

I said nothing more. We obviously had two different views of the matter, and mine was simple. You don't take advantage of a man, and you don't lie to him. Had she been going hungry without money to buy food, her effort to feed herself wherever and however she could would have been understandable, even acceptable, but she was implying, promising, by her willingness to look as beautiful for him as she possibly could and accompany him to an expensive dinner, that she was interested in him in a romantic and sexual way—and she was lying to him, letting him hope for something that would never happen, because she was never going to fulfill her implied promise.

# Chapter 15

# Meeting Doug

**I met my husband in 1979,** when I was 26. The six months right before we met were a period between my romantic entanglements when I had just declined a marriage proposal but I was still seeing the man as a friend. During those months a girlfriend began nagging me to go to clubs with her, which I repeatedly refused to do. I intensely disliked being in any type of bar or club. I have been in a grand total of maybe five in my life—and only because someone dragged me there.

As an aficionado of intelligent conversation with small numbers of intelligent people in intelligent surroundings, my idea of a good time has never been screaming (to be heard over the noise) at some idiot I can barely see through the smoke that's choking me to death. Even worse, the '70s were the days of disco, and disco and my preferred rock bands (the Doors, Bob Seger, Creedence Clearwater Revival) did *not* go together. Furthermore, since most people go to bars to drink, smoke, do drugs, or pick up bed partners, and I did none of that, I had no reason to go there.

At least once a week she nagged me then followed her nagging with the same impatient questioning of my constant refusal: "How do you expect to meet men?"

I explained that I did not want the kind of man who frequented that environment, and besides, I wasn't worried about meeting men because any man I was supposed to meet would walk up to my door and knock on it. I did not have to leave my apartment to meet a man.

She ridiculed this as "living in a fantasy world of prince charming rescuing the maiden."

I explained it was the pattern of my life, the way in which I had always met the men I was supposed to meet. I told her to just wait and watch, and I would prove it to her. And I did. Over the next six months, six different men walked up to my door and knocked on it.

**Man #1** was trying to sell me magazines when he abruptly stopped in the middle of his spiel and said, "Ahh, I don't want to sell you these things, I want to ask you to dinner." I laughed, but I declined, even after he assured me that he was a perfectly normal guy, and he had never before asked out anyone he was trying to sell to.

**Man #2** was a serial rapist, who doesn't actually qualify as a potential suitor, but he showed up at my door during that time period; therefore, technically I have to include him.

I did not know his vocation or that he was out practicing it when he arrived on a sunny Saturday afternoon asking if I knew where "so and so" lived. All I knew was that a large, soft,

"non-violent" man (in the sense that he avoided beatings and bru-
tality) with a pouring need to have women love him was standing
at my door. I knew better than to fall for the old telephone trick,
yet, despite that, I told him—when he asked if he could use my
phone to "call the people he was trying to locate"—that he could
come in only if he promised not to beat me up and rape me.

He acquired this abrupt stunned look and said, "But . . . I
don't even have a gun."

I started to say, "As big as you are, you wouldn't need one,"
but caught myself in time, and substituted, "You have to promise.
Are you going to promise or not?"

He promised, and I stood in the open doorway, intending to
run outside if he made even one gesture at me, while he went into
the other room, made his phony phone call (that even I knew was
to Time and Temperature), acted hesitant about something, then
left. A couple of days later, he returned late at night, pretending
he wanted me to make some of the pillows for him that he had
seen in my apartment. I barely cracked the door open, was icy
cold to him, kept the chain on, and kept my shoulder ready to
slam the door shut and lean into it while I hastily locked it. He
left and never returned. A few weeks later, I learned that a man
fitting his unique description had raped about 15 young, single
women in our complex, using the telephone ruse.

Years later, a girlfriend told me that she was in another country when a man tried assaulting her, and she, remembering how
I had made a serial rapist promise not to rape me, drew herself
up and righteously said, "You can't do this to me. I'm a citizen of
the United States of America." Her attacker halted dead still in
his tracks in an effort to puzzle out the reason she had given him

for why he could not carry out his assault, and while he tried to decipher it, she escaped.

I've often wondered what purpose my tiny little interchange played in the evolutionary journey and personal development of the rapist who came to my door. I intuitively knew that he raped to carry out a fantasy that many women loved him. By using his massive strength and weight to hold them still so that they could not struggle, he pretended they were cooperating, and he deluded himself that because he didn't use violence (knives, guns, beatings), he wasn't "forcing." I made him promise not to do that, and though he hesitated, he held to it.

On the other hand, maybe he just didn't want to have to deal with me standing there yelling like a kid, "You *promised*, you big liar. I'll *never* trust you again, you big fat liar."

**Man #3 and Man #4** were both neighbors who had seen me around. I declined them too, although I had an interesting interchange with **Man #3**, who first knocked on my door at ten o'clock one freezing evening. I cracked it open (chain fully in place) to find a man I had never set eyes on, claiming to be my neighbor and issuing a dinner invitation. I declined courteously through the two inches of open space around my door; then I shut it and shot the lock back in place.

A few days later, I ran into him in the parking lot and discovered he actually *was* my neighbor, and he was now worried that I thought he was Jack the Ripper. I did not bother to tell him that Jack had already shown up. Instead, we talked enough for me to see he really was a normal person. I had less than zero sexual attraction to him (and thus less than zero romantic interest), but I told him that I was up for occasional conversation as long as he understood there could never be any sex or romance. (I always spelled that out instantly to avoid undercurrents and misunderstandings.)

He invited me to his place for dinner and a game of Scrabble, all the while promising me that he was an excellent cook, but after I agreed, he began acting strangely unsettled and finally burst out that he "had something to tell me" that "scared off women."

I thought, *Now you mention it?* Yet all I said was, "Okay, out with it."

He told me that he kept pet snakes. I said, "Big ones?" He said, yes, very large ones.

I said, "In cages?" He said, yes, very secure cages, and he let them out only when people were not there.

I had to think it over because I had grown up in copperhead country, and no one there messed with copperheads unless they were dumb enough to think the Good Lord wanted them to "take up serpents" to prove their faith, but after he assured me that his snakes were not cobras, copperheads, or cottonmouths, I finally said, "Okay, I can handle it as long as they're in cages."

His apartment was a one-bedroom flat with the living room in the front and the dining area and kitchen at the rear. The snakes dwelled in his living room; therefore, to get to the dinner table I had to pass through a roomful of snakes. He courteously escorted me on a slow, investigative walk around the room that allowed me to examine each glass cage and ascertain that the tops were secure enough to make me feel secure. Then we reached his kitchen, and I discovered this guy meant it when he said he liked to cook. His fully equipped kitchen included a wall hung with every style of knife and meat cleaver that could be purchased.

There I was, with a total stranger, sandwiched in between a wall full of meat cleavers and a roomful of snakes, knowing that if I ever had to make a run for it, I would have to sprint past the snakes, and for all I knew, he had those things trained to lurch out of their cages at the sound of a whistle. His living room furniture was upholstered in a black and white plaid, and the stripes in the plaid were about the size of a good, healthy snake. So, I sat at his dining table, trying to act comfortable and converse in a normal tone while keeping watch over him, the meat cleavers, the snakes, and the plaid sofa, and privately swearing that out of the corner of my eye, I could see those stripes moving.

I began repeating to myself: "This is a normal man who has lived a normal life. He has two beloved teenage daughters from a previous marriage. He has a master's degree in biochemistry and he holds a senior level management position at a large company. This is a normal man . . ."

He was a good cook and a good conversationalist, and believe it or not, I actually got comfortable around those snakes—not that I was playing tag with them or anything, but I got comfortable enough to forget we were in the same room together.

He and I remained strictly, rigidly platonic right to the end. He went on a lot of lengthy business trips, and he asked me to go in and feed and water his guinea pig while he was gone. I was nervous the first time, afraid the stripes on that plaid upholstery were the snakes "a laying for me," but eventually I was able to go in by myself and not fear the snakes. He was highly defensive about all snakes, said it was terrible the way they were treated when they were so vulnerable with their long, thin bodies stretched out on the ground, and he was right. I even began to sympathize with the snakes and lose a great deal of the fear I had absorbed as a child. In this manner, he gave me something I needed at that time, and I remember him with a degree of fondness.

**Man #5** was a friend of another of my neighbors. He walked up to me as I was cleaning out my car and introduced himself with a unique opener: "You are a lot better looking than your car."

Whether he meant that as a compliment or an insult is still a mystery. No one has ever been able to interpret it. When he asked me out, I smiled and replied that we were not suited for each other. He told me that I was totally crazy, that I had never seen him before in my entire life and, therefore, it was impossible for me to know that we were not suited. I told him that I was an excellent judge of male energy, his and mine were not and would never be complementary, and to go out with him was to imply otherwise. He plopped down on the grass and sprawled back and said—with dead seriousness, for he was not trying to be funny— that he couldn't believe he wanted to go out with someone as crazy as I was.

He had just come from a tennis game, and he was wearing only a pair of shorts and shoes. So, while I continued cleaning my car, he sat in the sunshine with sweat pouring off his bare chest and tried to convince me, a crazy woman, to go out with him, a perfectly sane man. I was sitting in the driver's seat of my car, cleaning the dashboard, but the door was open so that I could reach the cleaning equipment sitting on the pavement. After I had told him at least 30 times that I would not go out with him, he, utterly oblivious to how I might react, squatted down beside my car door and thoughtfully confided to me (and with an innocent belief that I would fully agree and understand) that he was "sick and tired of liberated women" and he thought we ought to go back to "me Tarzan, you Jane." I fell forward across the steering wheel in a state of unending laughter that any man would be honest enough to say that to a total stranger with whom he was trying to get a date.

Well, I liked him. I really, really liked him. I still like him, and I am very grateful to him for his brash ways, because the friend he was visiting that day was an exceptionally reserved man who would have done almost anything before he would have walked up to me the way his brash friend did, but his friend broke the ice for him and that altered everything, which brings me to the one I was meant to meet.

**Man #6** was the friend that **Man #5** was visiting, and on July 4, 1979, about six months after I had told my girlfriend that if a man were out there that I was supposed to meet, I could sit in my apartment and never leave it, and he would walk up to my door and knock on it, I was busy at my sewing machine, making a red halter top, when Doug walked over and knocked on my door.

He has since owned the keys to all my doors.

And my girlfriend?

She said bluntly: "I don't believe this. If I had not seen this, I never would have believed it."

I said: "I told you so."

# Chapter 16
# Dougisms

My husband, Doug, should have been a stand-up comedian. He has the funniest, fastest, most genuine wit of any person I have ever known. His humor is not sarcasm or ridiculous lunacy or denigration of others or bathroom jokes, and he never needs four-letter words for emphasis. His humor is based in his perceptive ability to recognize the absurdity of everyday situations and his instantaneous ability to verbalize a countering response. I call them "Dougisms," and I am happy to share a few of my favorites in this chapter.

**Anecdote #1:** We were out driving one day when we passed a billboard that advertised a package of Winston cigarettes with the slogan: "Finally, A Butt You Can Kiss."

Doug said thoughtfully, "If I were the Cancer Society, I would rent the other side of that billboard and put up a sign that said, "Smoke These, And You Can Kiss Your Butt Goodbye."

**Anecdote #2:** One Saturday morning, while having coffee and reading the newspaper, I came across an article about a man who had become so angry at a dog that he had viciously bit the dog—really tore out a hunk of fur and flesh—forcing the dog to be hospitalized. I read this story out loud while grimacing and curling my face to dramatize my nausea at gulping down an unsanitary mouthful of fur, fleas, and whatever the dog had rolled in.

Doug looked up questioningly from his sports page and asked, "Well? Are they going to put that man to sleep?"

**Anecdote #3:** I was reading about some people being stranded in the wilderness, which got me wondering who I would want with me should I ever be in that position. I instantly chose Doug, and I told him why—because his highly inventive nature would substantially increase our chances of surviving.

I then asked who he would prefer to be stranded with, expecting of course, that he would say, "My darling, if I am going to be stranded in the wilderness, doomed to die in horrible circumstances, then the last sight I want to see is your lovely face."

Here's what he actually said, and he said it so fast that you would suspect he had already thought about it many times before: "You. Because of your extreme survival instinct and your tenacity and calmness in bad situations. Also, you don't eat meat. So I know that when we run out of food, you won't kill me and eat me."

**Anecdote #4:** Years ago, Doug knew a female architect who, as a committed Roman Catholic, was determined to remain a virgin until she married a fellow Roman Catholic, who was, preferably, also a virgin, but if not, he must not have been married (and thus divorced). She was a quite attractive woman, ambitious and somewhat brusque, but basically nice.

She went on a vacation to Europe, and while there, in a nation universally known for its Lotharios, she was approached by a man who wanted to bed her. She rejected him. He attempted to persuade her to engage in an intimate fling by claiming he was a unique opportunity that she would never again be able to take advantage of. He told her that if she were visiting a city she would never again visit and she saw the most beautiful and perfectly made pair of shoes that she would never find anywhere else, she would buy those shoes, because, if she didn't, they would be out of her reach forever. He was that pair of shoes.

As she recounted this to her friends and coworkers and struggled mightily to convey the extremity of her outrage and contempt, her appalled horror at the Lothario's reasoning, and her monumental disbelief that any man would compare sexual intercourse with her as equivalent to buying a pair of shoes, Doug glanced up and matter-of-factly stated the perfect double entendre comeback: "You should have told him that he was not your size."

**Anecdote #5:** Back in the late 1970s a singer named Johnny Paycheck had a gigantic hit with a song called "Take This Job and Shove It, I Ain't Working Here No More." This song was such a huge hit because it resonated with everyone across all levels of society who worked a job they did not like but needed to pay their bills.

Before Johnny became a country singing star, he had spent some time in the joint, and after he became a star, he apparently did not see any reason to change his ways. So, sometime in the 1980s he ended up back in the slammer for trying to shoot someone in a bar in Hillsboro, Ohio.

A few years later, long about 1991, Doug and I were in the bathroom one evening, getting ready for bed. He was in the shower, and I was at the sink brushing my teeth, thus my mouth was crammed full of paste, foam, and water—an important component to what happened next.

Doug turned off the shower and opened the curtain, and he was standing there silently drying off when he suddenly drawled, "Well . . . I heard today they're letting that Johnny Paycheck back out on the streets. I suppose his next song will be 'Take This Jail and Shove It, I Ain't Making License Plates Here No More.'"

I spewed paste, foam, and water all over that sink.

**Anecdote #6:** Doug's ability to say these things without cracking a smile is not limited to those moments when the rest of us can freely laugh out loud. He himself doesn't laugh at what he says, which means that he can say them during highly formal moments and stand there acting all dignified while the rest of us are jouncing around like break dancers in an effort to control our bodily functions.

Back in the late 1980s, he and I were attending a private showing of the artwork in the Son of Heaven exhibit that was touring the nation. This exhibit covered about 2,600 years of artwork from an ancient Chinese culture that had worshipped their emperors as the "Son of Heaven," believing them to be the human link to heaven. Much of this art had been found in some remote area of China, and these mesmerizing pieces included items from the palaces of Chinese emperors, scroll paintings, a jade burial suit, a throne, and life-sized terra-cotta sculptures of warriors and horses.

A cocktail party preceded this private showing. Now, I intensely dislike cocktails parties (which I privately call Corncob Parties because everyone stands around so stiff and uneasy as if they have corncobs up their rears), and I am proud to say that in my time, I have undergone inimitable social gyrations in order to avoid them. However, I was at this one because the private showing that followed the social hour enabled us to leisurely take our time going through the exhibit with just a few quiet people (fellow architects who knew something about art) instead of being rushed through with mobs of noisy people as would occur at a public showing.

As part of the sensitive, artistic community of Columbus, Ohio, we were all standing around as if we had just had fresh corncobs installed, eating shrimp off those stingy little plates that never hold as much as you really want. The men were all sheathed in dark suits, the women in little black dresses (the sensitive and artistic can be highly creative with color), and with all that black and everyone all somber and sober, you would have guessed we had convened there to honor some recently deceased acquaintance with a shrimp meal.

Then came time for the tour. Because this artwork was so ancient and, in many respects, fragile and sensitive to light and sound, the museum had placed the artwork in carpeted and dimly lit rooms. With all of us in black—somber, sober, corncobs firmly in place—we strongly resembled a funeral procession shuffling through those rooms.

Doug and I had fallen in beside two acquaintances, Brian and Cheryl, and the four of us had progressed about a third of the way through the exhibit when we entered a section of truly astonishing, deeply ceremonial, religious artifacts that were about 2,500 years old.

The first artifacts were an entire set of 26 huge, heavy, thick, bronze temple bells, hanging off a set of rigid steel bars, positioned parallel to the floor. The bells had been hung according to size, smallest to the largest, in a perfect formation of three neat rows, and it had surely taken heavy moving equipment to heft those things up on those bars. Nearby, perched high on a platform and beautifully lit, were two gigantic ceremonial urns, also bronze and probably four feet tall and another three to four feet across—an eight-year-old child could have bathed in one of them without bumping the sides. The handles of huge ladles extended out of these urns. We were told they had been used for preparing special ceremonial foods while the bells were sounded during rituals honoring the Son of Heaven.

We gazed on this from a state of motionless awe, immersed in the dimly lit, cathedral-like atmosphere of this ancient culture's adoration of the Son of Heaven, each of us withdrawn inside ourselves as we silently marveled at the sight of those 26 gigantic bronze bells, standing before us in a ramrod formation of perfect rows.

Into this respectful hush, Doug unexpectedly stage-whispered: "The Son of Heaven's Marching Band."

Brian, Cheryl and I underwent an entire series of uncontrolled bodily contortions and choking, muffled, snorting throat noises in response to the incongruous image of an ancient Chinese culture lugging around those insanely heavy bells during some ceremony while they blared "Hang On Sloopy, Sloopy Hang On . . ." all to the glorious honor of the Son of Heaven.

Doug, oblivious to the potential danger to us of voicing his insights into great art, turned his gaze onto those two giant urns with the big ladles sticking out of them and stage-whispered, "The Son of Heaven's Chili Cookoff."

Without going into a lot of detail, I will say only that at least the guards did not throw us out.

# Chapter 17
# Of Mice and Computers

Anyone who bought a personal computer back during the 1980s or 1990s—I got my first in 1985—still has nightmare memories of how hundreds of different programs were competing for dominance, none of them were compatible, bugs inhabited every nook and cranny, and the few people who knew how to correct the most minor of computer problems had gone into hiding from the millions of us who were hunting them down for assistance.

My first computer was an IBM-XT, which used the Wordstar word processing program and the large five-by-five-inch floppy disks. That machine was perfection. In the nine years I used it, it never had one single hardware or software problem, which an experienced and disbelieving technician told me was unheard of in any computer. I loved it so much that I was unable to give it up, and even after I replaced it, I kept it beside me for a full year before I finally stored it safely in a box and gave it an honored position in my sewing room, where it still is. My XT's only flaw was that its two floppy drives—confidently recommended by the salesman, who was unaware of how fast I can type—were incapable of storing the massive amount of writing that I generate.

About a week after my purchase, I was zipping through those big floppies by the dozens. During the spring of 1987, a computer tech friend replaced one of my floppy drives with a hard drive, all the time offering brisk assurance that the hard drive had so much storage capability (640K) that I would *never* use all that memory.

Now . . . anyone who has been on the receiving end of one of my 500-page, single-spaced letters or 1,000-page, single-spaced manuscripts can testify under oath that 640K is the equivalent of one long sentence for me. I told him, "It's not large enough. I'll fill it within six months."

And I did. Just weeks later, I was back to buying floppies in bulk. Normal people bought them 10 to a box, but I found a place that sold them 50 at a time in a big plastic bag, and I stocked up about once every two weeks.

After nine years of use, my perfect, trusty XT was hopelessly outdated, and I was forced to buy a second computer. When I asked our friend how much hard memory I should get, he said, "For you? Start with at least a gigabyte. Not a K less."

My second computer in 1996 was an unmitigated and unapologetic chunk of junk that introduced me to the two universal problems that were the bane of computer users during those years: incompetent telephone technical support and inability to get online using AOL software. After two years spent struggling with both, I concluded that anyone possessing a trace of human DNA could get a job designing AOL software or answering calls for tech support.

When I asked our tech friend why I had to reload my AOL every two or three days, he told me the disk was possibly bad, but the street rap about AOL among "his kind" (computer techs) was that the software itself was total junk, he personally had nothing good to say about it, and I should opt for a different online service.

During that same time period, I happened across a *MAD* magazine satire that claimed to have planted a spy inside the telephone tech support offices, who had uncovered a secret memo of 10 training instructions that told the techs how to deal with all telephone callers.[1] Among those 10 items were these absolutely true gems, which, except for number five, I have paraphrased:

1. When customers have hardware problems, blame their software.
2. When customers have software problems, blame their hardware.
3. If you have no idea what the problem is, tell customers they need an upgrade.
4. Tell them their other programs are not compatible with yours.
5. "AOL is the official scapegoat for any hardware or software problem a customer may experience. AOL has screwed up so much over the last two years that anybody will accept AOL as the cause of their problem—even if they don't have AOL."

---

[1] "The 10 Rules of Computer Tech Support," *MAD*, February 1999, pgs 30-31.

In fairness, I sympathize with all computer technicians, because computer ignorance among lay people makes their job extremely difficult. I would never inflict some of my acquaintances onto any computer technician, especially the female friend, who, while intoxicated, called the techs for help and proceeded to inform the poor guy who got stuck taking her call that her problem with her computer was that she "lacked a gun to shoot the damn thing."

Technicians can tell hilarious stories about their experiences and the amount of patient restraint they have needed to cope with the lack of simple understanding they have encountered in people. Two memorable tales that stand out in my memory are the woman who thought "using windows" meant she was to relocate her computer near the building's windows, and the fastidious man who thoroughly scrubbed his keyboard at the kitchen sink, then blamed the company he bought it from that it no longer worked.

Still, this ignorance goes both ways, and I can top any story any tech tells with the following story of the ignorance I have encountered in technicians.

Just after I bought my chunk-of-junk second computer, I underwent the following real-life, word for word exchanges with telephone technical support personnel, and I am *not* making these up. I always recorded (and still do) every tiny detail of any problem that occurs with my computers along with all related conversations, and I swear to you that these are true, *word for actual word*:

**Third Place Prize Goes To:**
Technical Support: "And what is your problem?"

Me: "My computer will not boot up when I turn it on."

Technical Support: "So? Don't turn it on."

**Second Place Prize Goes To:**

Technical Support: "And what is your problem?"

Me: "My computer will not boot up when I turn it on, and if it does boot up, and I turn it off, then I can't get it to boot up again."

Technical Support: "Well, don't turn it off."

**First Place Grand Prize Goes To** (and this is *word for word exactly what was said*)**:**

Technical Support: "And what is your problem?"

Me: "My computer will not boot up when I turn it on, and if it does boot up, and I turn it off, I can't get it to boot up again."

Technical Support: "Are there any dead animals in it?"

Me: "Umm . . . what exactly do you mean?"

Technical Support: "Are mice living in it?"

Me: "Umm . . . are you asking if my computer mouse is working properly . . . or are you referring to the actual animal?"

Technical Support: "Yes, the animal. Sometimes mice start living in them and that can interfere."

Me: "I've recently had a technician look in my machine, and I'm certain that if I had any animals there, living or dead, he would have found them and informed me."

I finally terminated weeks of the above helpful advice by calling a local company and hiring a tech to visit my home. I warned the man who took my call: "Don't send me a bonehead. I am in no mood to deal with another bonehead."

He obligingly said: "I promise I will not send you a bonehead."

His fulfillment of that promise led to an eventual resolution of the problem, which was, of course, to buy a new computer from an entirely different company, one that was not constantly changing its name and moving around the country to stay ahead of our state's Attorney General who was trying to track them down for defrauding customers.

As naïve as it may sound, by the time that "animals living in your computer" comment was said to me, I had heard so many unintelligent statements from telephone tech support that I honestly just took it in stride, accepted it as a "normal" theory, and tried reasoning with it in a matter-of-fact manner.

Then Doug got hold of it.

He stared at me for a few seconds before he slowly shook his head and said, "Oh, man! If they think that rodents in your computer are the source of your problems, they have no idea what they are doing, and they'll believe anything. You should have said, 'Well . . . I do have this big groundhog living in there, but Fred swears to me that he doesn't touch a thing, so I let him stay.'"

# Chapter 18

# A Drive in the Country

Doug is the kind of man a woman likes to have around, because, when he decides to do that "man thing" of insisting on having his way, it's always what we women want too—dinners out, vacations, and new clothes.

Before we escaped the city of Columbus to these woods where we now live, he would sometimes come home from work and say, "You spend too much time in this house. You need to get out. Make a reservation at The Refectory." (A high-priced, high-quality restaurant about 10 minutes from where we lived.) I would always say, "No, no, I'm fine. Really." He would say, "I insist," and I, knowing it was useless to argue with such a bull-headed man, would just get up and go pick up the phone and make the call.

One time he came home and said, "Let's go somewhere far away. An island." I said, "That will be expensive." He said, "I insist." I said, "Okay, you win. How about this one?" and whipped out a clipping of an intriguing little Caribbean island called Saba that I had cut from the newspaper's travel section just two days before.

Back in February 1999, he began insisting that we take a vacation. And for some reason he himself could not explain, he wanted me to choose our destination without any input from him, even though we always selected our vacation sites by agreeing on some generalized destination (such as an island), then narrowing it to a specific place.

I was in the mood for something remote and isolated, but the moon was not a feasible choice, so I suggested northern Maine as a reasonable substitute. He said fine. Since September is our preferred month for vacations—because the weather is neither hot nor cold and the tourist crowds have gone home to put their noisy kids back in school—I had plenty of time to research Maine and structure our limited vacation time along routes that included the most interesting sites.

Yet as the weeks passed, I kept avoiding doing any research and making any plans until finally I asked myself, "Do I even want to take a vacation?"

I answered, "Yes, but this won't be a vacation. It will be meeting deadlines—flights, rental cars, hotel reservations, and destinations before we hurry on to more flights, hotels, and destinations."

So I said to myself, "I have 10 days to take off somewhere. What do I *want* to do?"

I answered, "I want to put my credit cards in one pocket and a thousand dollars in the other, sling a canteen of water over my shoulder, throw a gym bag full of essentials into the backseat of our car, and just start driving. No deadlines, no flights, no rental cars, no hotel reservations, no opening and closing times for museums, no anything. Just Doug and me and the road."

When Doug came home that day, I, knowing my new vacation plan did not sound vibrant or exciting—thus expecting some resistance from him—waited for an agreeable moment to suggest that we not fly anywhere but instead, just take a drive through three of Ohio's neighboring states. He simply shrugged and said he didn't care where we went, but we had to go somewhere and get away for a while. Another day went by, which is how long it took me to realize I was still dreading our trip, dreading the very thought of racing along interstates at high speed to fit pre-chosen destinations from three states into 10 short days, when all I wanted to do was coast through a countryside filled with meadow-covered hills and valleys, lounge on the grassy banks of hidden lakes, munch fruit, cheese and bread, and wash it all down with a slurp from a canteen while gazing at the sky for no productive reason.

So, when Doug arrived home, I warily met him with a new and far more restricted plan for our 10-day respite (one that I was confident would get more reaction from him than a dismissive shrug): "Uhhhh . . . I would like to limit our drive to the southwestern quadrant of Ohio."

For at least a full minute, he stood there gazing at me in a contemplative manner until I finally added kind of wryly, "I know. If I keep limiting this, we'll never leave the living room."

He said: "Yeah. I was just thinking we could take Route 23 out of Columbus for about a mile, park alongside the road, and sit in the car for a week."

I said: "Here's my problem. All we do is meet deadlines in our work, and I want 10 days of freedom from deadlines. I want to cruise along backroads through small towns, eat in places no one has ever heard of and may not want to hear of, and stay in little bed-and-breakfast inns that are 300 years old and have signs out front that say "George Washington Slept Here" or "Daniel Boone Killed a Bear Right Over There."

For another full minute, Doug's gaze remained unwaveringly fixed on me, certain that this would be the most unimaginative and dreary vacation he had ever taken, but since his only way out of a trip that he had insisted I design was to inform me that he would now take command because my brain was obviously malfunctioning—not a wise move by any husband anywhere—he finally nodded his agreement. Then, throughout the months before our departure date arrived, he also did his best to warm to my plan by never once voicing his doubts or questioning my choice.

So it came to pass that in 1999, as August drifted into September, we loaded his pickup truck with water, food and travel bags, climbed in, and embarked on an exploration of the backroads and small towns in Ohio's southwestern quadrant.

## The Southwestern Quadrant

Although I was born in southeastern Ohio, and Doug was born in central Ohio, neither of us had ever seen more of the southwestern quadrant than the glimpses we had ignored while on the interstate between Cincinnati (perched on the southern edge of the state) and Columbus (smack in the center). The meandering, circular course I charted avoided the interstates and the big cities and allowed us to cruise slowly through the Ohio countryside, visit the ancient Indian Mounds built by the Hopewell and Adena cultures as far back as 3,000 years ago, lounge on the banks of obscure rivers and lakes, and sleep in a few bed-and-breakfast inns of historical significance.

Ohio has a deserved reputation for being populated with tiny burgs too small to have a traffic light or even a name (except nicknames known only to the locals), acres of farmland milling with sleepy, lumbering cows, and no especially startling or inviting features—no high mountains or painted deserts—although we do have Lake Erie. You just have to drive up to Canada to find it. So, I was a bit leery of my own vacation choice, but to our delight, each day of our road trip was so individualized that after traveling only 15 to 25 miles we would enter an environment unlike any of the previous ones.

After 10 days we returned home from the most refreshing vacation we had ever taken, immensely satisfied with a driving trip that had been lazy, undemanding, and filled with a string of quirky delights—a cave containing a rock formation nicknamed "Daniel Boone and His Coonskin Cap," a village with the perfectly unsophisticated name of Knockemstiff, a house where someone of questionable aesthetics had used leftover siding to fill in the obvious site of a former front door, giving the house the bizarre appearance of having a sealed mouth, and a place called Rabbit Hash, where two dogs chained to an ancient, dilapidated barn leaped and barked wildly upon spotting us in their crazed effort to alert any visible human that the barn was sure to collapse on their heads and make Dog Hash out of them. Down in Maysville, Kentucky, just across the Ohio River from Ripley, a restaurant menu listed fried frog legs served with rice and vegetables as a "Regional Favorite." We were asked, "Where you folks from?" probably 500 times, I was called "hon" (short for "honey") approximately 150 times, and memorable signs hailed us everywhere we went:

At a driveway gate: "If I'm not here to greet you, you shouldn't be here."

On the door of an antique store: "Open Friday and Saturday, other times by chance."

At the Decatur Cemetery: "A Lasting Tribute."

At a bend in a driveway: "Your last chance to get the hell out of here before I throw you out."

On a fence: "Trespassers will be shot. Survivors will be shot again."

## Bed-and-Breakfast

For any reader who does not know, the entire southern border of Ohio is the Ohio River, which separates Ohio from Kentucky and West Virginia. The Ohio River Valley was a hotbed of abolitionist activity prior to the "Rebel War" (as the locals called it when I was a child growing up there, though it's more commonly known as the Civil War). The Ohio River was the border between the northern free states and the southern slave states, and being a large, dangerous river, it was also a major obstacle that runaway slaves had to cross. About every third house along the river can tell a tale (and often it's even true) of having been part of that Underground Railroad "route to freedom" that funneled fugitive slaves into northern states and on up to Canada.

Before we departed on our trip, I made four reservations at B&Bs to ensure a place to stay in the villages of rural areas where the inhabitants—if you could find any—would either laugh or question your intelligence if you asked for directions to the local motel. Three of these B&Bs were houses that were 150 to 200 years old, places so old they had housed both fugitive slaves and the general (Ulysses S. Grant) who had led the Union Army during the Civil War. Sleeping overnight in old houses that have a rowdy or unsettled history always rouses a certain caution in me. Such places crawl with the astral presences of yesteryear's now deceased occupants who always eagerly pounce on anyone on the physical plane with whom they can communicate. I did not want to end up like Whoopi Goldberg in the movie *Ghost*.

My bigger concern, however, was in not knowing what we might be getting in a bed-and-breakfast. Their promotional materials are as slick and trustworthy as an icy sidewalk, and too often, someone else's idea of "charming Victorian" in some quaint village is my version of "badly in need of renovation and a good cleaning." I opted for B&Bs anyhow, out of my robust, though quite possibly ill-conceived eager determination to cling to a fragile idea of undertaking this trip in a happy spirit of shared adventure, like Huck Finn and Jim, scooting down the Mississippi on a raft.

The first B&B room that I reserved was in Ripley, down on the Ohio River, a house which, in about 1838, had boarded a young student of no noticeable potential by the name of Ulysses S. Grant. The owner was halfway clearing her throat when she spoke to me on the telephone, and she sort of "swallowed" the fee she charged per night.

All I heard was "five dollars," which silenced me for probably ten seconds while I thought: *How can anyone run an inn for five dollars per night?* Followed rapidly by: *Oh God, what kind of dump am I getting us into? Does she think that B&B stands for Blanket and Board Floor?*

I recovered, reasoned I surely had not heard the full information, took a halfway educated guess at the price, based on what the fees were running in the travel guidebook I was consulting, and said, "Umm . . . did you say sixty-five?"

She replied, "No, seventy-five," which was joyous news. If she had said a hundred and seventy-five, I would have paid it just to know we would be assigned to an actual room complete with a bed.

So, with four B&B reservations in place (the only four deadlines we had to meet), and expecting to easily find all other accommodations in various motels along the way, Doug and I departed Columbus one early morning in the early autumn of 1999 and drove southwest, naively determined to trust our guidebook and follow the roads less travelled that were clearly marked on our newly purchased Ohio road map. We did not yet know that our map had been drawn by someone who was unaware that travelers hoped to use it for navigating the state's highways and byways—mostly byways in our case—and our guidebook had been written, not by some curious and plucky explorer recounting bona fide experiences and personally authenticated investigations, but by a dull sluggard who had never hoisted himself off his couch long enough to visit even one of the historical sites and bed-and-breakfast inns whose attributes he so vividly and falsely described.

**Friday, Day 1: The Hopewell Mounds**

I must mention here at the start, because of what happened days later when we reached the Great Serpent Mound, that a terrible bout of insomnia afflicted me during the two nights before we left home. Launching our trip in the midst of an influx of force that was battering my body and preventing me from sleeping was admittedly a questionable decision, but this was a vacation I had been looking forward to, and I was determined to take it even if I had to stagger through it in utter exhaustion from lack of sleep.

Our first stop before reaching the Hopewell Mounds was at a wilderness site that our guidebook had enthusiastically promoted as having a "parking lot" from which a "well-marked trail" led to a fabulous "scenic view" of some gorgeous "whatever you do, don't miss these" cliffs, and it was here, without venturing one step further into our trip, that we learned our guidebook's author had just taken a wild guess as to the nature of the various sites that he recommended. The "parking lot" was a gravel berm, barely wide enough for someone needing to pull over and fix a flat tire and completely unable to accommodate a horde of tourists, which, fortunately, it would never need to do. This "parking lot" extended about 20 feet down the side of an isolated road that bordered a wall of brush that could be penetrated only by chopping through it with a sickle.

We parked, taking up half the "lot," and optimistically hunted around for the starting point of a trail, which we found after we unearthed the trail's faded "closed" sign, pressed flat into the ground and almost fully buried under brush. The closed sign was no longer necessary—the trees and poison ivy had overgrown the trail and closed it years before—but we dug up the sign and dragged it out of the brush anyhow, then propped it beside a large information board, whose rusted metal posts clung grimly to their upright position in order to announce officiously: "Map On

Back." The reverse side contained an ink line that some helpful visitor had contributed—much appreciated, but useless, as the single scrawled line corresponded to nothing identifiable.

Still, we gamely thrust aside the bushes and weeds, side-stepped the trees, and gingerly penetrated the woods a few feet before deciding that getting hopelessly lost on a non-existent trail was not worth any "fabulous scenic view." Call us suspicious, but we suspected our guidebook's description of the view was as truthful as "parking lot" and "well-marked trail." We retreated to our pickup truck, startled to discover that in our brief absence another truck identical to Doug's had soundlessly materialized on this isolated country road and filled the remaining 10-foot stretch in the "parking lot." The soundless arrival was a bit unnerving, as we had gone only a few feet into the woods and should have heard the truck's engine, but to our delight, the driver looked a lot like Doug, even more so than Doug's own brother does.

Doug greeted the stranger with a cordial: "Nice looking vehicle you have, and we even resemble each other. About the same age, beard, glasses . . ."

The other man stared at us in utter silence from narrowed, suspicious eyes as if we resembled escaped felons he had been tracking, and Doug abruptly halted in mid-sentence and bid the stranger a hearty goodbye. The man still said nothing. After we were locked inside our pickup and safely back on the road, and I could keep a lookout over my shoulder to see if we were being tailed, I asked: "Why did you stop? Did he make you uneasy?"

Doug said: "Not exactly. I started to add 'and we both need to lose a few pounds,' but I stopped in case our resemblance did not include both of us having a sense of humor."

After abandoning this public park disappointment, we drove southward to Chillicothe, home of the Hopewell Indian Mounds. I had been there once before, by myself, during a cold December in 1974 when the park had been wisely deserted, although the bitter cold was not the only reason I was the only visitor. The bleak, deserted atmosphere was so warlike, destructive, negative, and depressing that those Mounds were no tourist magnet even during a hot summer. I had risked a tentative climb to the top of a rickety observation tower—after checking for a condemned sign—whose only merit was that it gave me a comprehensive view of the Mounds while I wondered how many years my corpse would lie undiscovered when that tower collapsed beneath me. I descended that trembling, dilapidated structure with even more cautious care than I had climbed it, and the very moment my feet hit the ground, I took a guess on which direction that tower might fall and sprinted the opposite way, intending never to return.

Twenty-five years later, Doug and I arrived together on a sunny, late summer day to be greeted by the inviting atmosphere of a picnic park and a modern visitor's center that had replaced the ramshackle observation tower. My previous negative reaction from 1974 bewildered me—as my intuitive perceptions have never been wrong—until I bought a slim guidebook and learned that the existing Mounds, for the most part, were a reconstruction of the original Mounds, which had been destroyed by a U.S. Army training camp erected during World War I. I had wrongly assumed in 1974 that the negativity and warlike destructiveness in the atmosphere was from the Mounds themselves, but it was actually the psychic residue from what had been done to the Mounds.

Razing the Mounds to install an Army training camp was an act of such astounding ignorance, selfishness, and contempt—the Army could have used the miles of relatively unpopulated land that surround the Mounds, negating all need for such senseless destruction—that Doug and I felt like gullible fools at seemingly approving the alteration by sauntering through and admiring the phony Indian Mounds the government had constructed to replace the real ones they had destroyed. Without any intelligent reason to continue approving government misconduct, we treated the visit as a history lesson and departed for a nearby museum, the Adena House and estate, the former home of a quite wealthy U.S. senator and Ohio governor who had owned thousands of acres of land and many prosperous businesses.

As we toured the Adena House, I intuited from the atmosphere that the land and house had been worked by black slaves. Although this contradicted what I knew about Ohio being a free state, I could not shed my certainty that the estate had been worked by slaves, which immediately aroused my "defense of the worker" persona, for slaves and servants have always been, to me, workers who have rights. I reacted with special intensity to the two rooms in the house most in need of good lighting and good air flow—the kitchen and the weaving room. The original owner had apparently believed it to be an excessive waste of a few dollars from his immense wealth to construct those crucial workrooms with proper lighting and air flow to relieve the dark gloom of short winter days or the immense heat that would have accumulated there in the summertime. Tiny openings barely lit those two critical work areas, yet the rest of the house—the owner's living quarters—contained unnecessarily gigantic windows. As we

174

passed through the kitchen, I again absorbed the atmosphere and knew (despite my intuitive certainty contradicting the physical facts of history) that he had not only used black slaves, he had also used white indentured servants.

The lack of lighting the owner had provided for his slaves and servants left me in a sour mood, and the previous two days of insomnia had eliminated my patience. I grumbled and muttered until Doug pointed out, "Glass was very expensive back then." I replied, "Yes, but for only two rooms? When all other rooms not in need of huge windows, contain huge windows? Furthermore, the cheap bastard found enough money to buy 5,000 acres of land and cover it with orchards and grain, and, according to this pamphlet, he also owned gristmills, sawmills, cattle companies, and river shipping all while prospecting for coal and iron."

Doug conceded my point, though he also mentioned judiciously that if I continued my churlish temper, I would have road rage after only one day of travel.

At the end of the tour, we entered a room containing a captioned and pictorial history of the people who had worked the estate along with a detailed account of how the owner had retained white indentured servants; he had also illegally brought black slaves to work the estate under the pretense that they too were indentured servants, thereby circumventing the laws against slavery.

Learning that the Ohio Historical Society had not whitewashed the truth lightened my mood considerably, and former Shawnee Chief Tecumseh lightened it further. Apparently, after being invited to the house for some undoubtedly useless political gathering, Tecumseh had declined sleeping in the guest bedroom and had slept instead, out on the lawn. The historians attributed this to his Indian nature, but I'm guessing the Chief had a few private thoughts about the company he was keeping.

**Chillicothe:** That evening we checked into our first bed-and-breakfast where we came face-to-face with one of the boldest of the bold lies from the indolent loafer who had authored our guidebook by relying on—just taking a guess here—promotional brochures, a telephone interview with the owners, or someone else's outdated guidebook. This B&B was the embodiment of the wretched lodgings I had envisioned and feared. It was an old Italianate house badly in need of a year's worth of extensive repairs and two years of industrial-level cleaning. The author's lengthy, glorifying review had not included the house's rundown condition or the mountainous layers of dust that coated its every interior surface. Old furniture, clothing, and knickknacks, caked and saturated with decades of ingrained dust and covered with loose layers of more recent dust, cluttered every room, including our upstairs bedroom and the downstairs kitchen and dining room. Although our bed linens were clean (and it was a relief to fold back those sheets and confirm the bed was not being colonized by an army of bugs), enough dust-choked Victorian clothes hung off the bedroom's furniture, walls and doors to launch a used clothing store.

If I had wanted to gaze upon racks of rumpled clothes, I would have stayed home and stared at my ironing, which was at least clean. But . . . we were Huck and Jim, adventuring, and all elements of our trip, whether good or bad, were part of our adventure and would not hamper our cheery determination to enjoy ourselves. So, we dropped our overnight cases on the bed—the only spot in the room clean enough to give us confidence that our belongings would not instantly vanish into some humongous dust dune—and departed to explore the town's historic district, examine the great old houses, visit antique shops, partake of a pleasant dinner at a restaurant, and stroll by another B&B that we wished I had chosen. The meticulously clean and beautifully maintained exterior implied that someone may have felt inspired to clean the interior too.

Upon returning to our unfortunate choice of lodgings, we trekked through the downstairs, being careful not to brush against anything and stir up clouds of dust, just to find, after climbing to our upstairs bedroom, that no waste basket had been provided for our used dental floss and tissues. No surprise really. I bagged our trash to take with us, but I could have left it on a dresser and by morning no one else could ever have found it—not that any cleaning service would have gone looking.

That night was hell. The antique bed was much shorter than Doug (I barely fit into it), which forced him to lie crumpled up for as long as he could tolerate it, then periodically thrash and twist in manifold ways in an effort to locate enough space to uncurl his legs. I could not fall asleep because I could not breathe. Somewhere around one a.m., I rolled out of bed and, using my travel flashlight, its beam dispersed by the dusty atmosphere into a smoky cloud of illumination, I rummaged through the room's closet in search of thick blankets I could use to bunk on the floor and give Doug the space to stretch out on the bed's diagonal. The closet surprised me with a folding cot that I gratefully hauled out and began erecting, cautiously, because I quickly discovered that hiding in that closet had not protected that cot, and unfolding it—even a gingerly inch by inch—was kicking up a dust storm worthy of 1930s Oklahoma. Finally, at about three a.m., out of the sheer physical exhaustion of holding my breath to avoid choking, I drifted into a half-awake sleep.

Sunrise and the opportunity to depart swept over us with the sweet feeling of freedom. We ate breakfast at the B&B, kept our complaints to ourselves, paid our bill and left a place we would never return to or recommend. Doug said he had awakened repeatedly all night and mistaken all those swaying Victorian clothes for headless people wandering around in our room. The worst and lasting consequence of that stay was the painful crick that Doug acquired in his neck from his accordion sleeping position of being scrunched up and unable to expand to his full body length. He carried that neck pain throughout our entire vacation because the stress of doing all the driving would not let it heal, and with my lack of sleep, I was in no condition to share the driving.

Doug was not eager to keep our reservations at the three remaining B&Bs, and my fervid assurances that B&Bs are highly individualized places did not ease his mind. The constant pain in his neck and the haunting memory of bodiless clothes floating through clouds of dust spoke more persuasively than I did.

## Saturday, Day 2: Seven Caves

**Knockemstiff:** As we left Chillicothe on our way toward Bainbridge, I persuaded Doug to detour through a village called Knockemstiff, a name so comical that I was determined to drop it into some future conversation, just a casual mention over dinner, "Yes . . . well, one day I was in Knockemstiff . . ."

That little detour provided us with our first realization that our Rand McNally map did not correspond with any actual roads in Ohio. Knockemstiff was not on the road the map claimed, nor was Knockemstiff on a nicely paved road as the map also claimed. We found Knockemstiff only after we abandoned a nicely paved road for a gravel road spread with tar, then left that for a rutted, dirt trail.

As we bounced wildly along the rutted trail, I informed Doug that unless our map was once again deceiving us, this rough stretch would not last long.

He said only, while grimly clutching the steering wheel: "Good. Because this road hasn't seen a car in a long while, and it doesn't know what to do with one."

Maybe Knockemstiff has grown since, but in 1999, it consisted of a few houses facing off like opponents preparing to fight over the ruts in the dirt trail that lay between them. We exchanged waves with some old codger as we simultaneously entered and departed Knockemstiff past a bewildering sign that one of its three or so residents had erected: "I am better than I was, but not quite as good as I was before I got worse."

That sign had to be referring to that road.

**Bainbridge** is distinguished by a beautiful rocky gorge called Seven Caves in which an enterprising robber by the name of Bob McKimie had hid out during the 1800s. The legend claims that ole' Bob hid . . . I think it was $10,000 or thereabouts in gold somewhere near the caves.

The gorge's name derives from being perforated by seven small caves, the kind that lead straight back into hillsides, the kind used by the bears that inhabited the area back in Bob's time. Most of the seven caves were more like small overhangs, but they were uniformly wired with lights that lit up specific portions of the caves, equipped with helpful little buttons we could push to turn the lights on, and studded with little plaques bearing names that conveyed what the cave formations resembled, such as "Elephant Ears."

Most of the tunnels leading into the caves were obligingly high and as much as four feet wide, allowing us to stand fully erect and saunter along, cheerfully pushing little buttons and trying, mostly without success, to detect the resemblance between the rocks and their given names. "Daniel Boone and His Coonskin Cap" stumped us completely. Only a resourceful imagination could ever detect Daniel Boone and his coonskin cap in that rock's shape, but since neither of us knew what Dan and his hat looked like to start with, we bowed to someone's superior knowledge and conceded the likeness.

The entrance to one cave bore a sign bearing the name "The Dungeon," along with a warning that the tunnel to it was "very low, very narrow, and for the young and nimble only."

The sign did not lie.

I led the way, crouched and hunched down like a troll. Some exceedingly narrow areas forced me to slide through sideways to avoid brushing against the grungy stone. We planned to stop for lunch afterwards, and I preferred not to look as if I had just staggered in from months of hiding out in a cave with Robber Bob.

About halfway down that passageway, claustrophobia abruptly and unexpectedly attacked me, something I had never before fallen prey to in previous caves, not even in tight spots. Genuine panic flashed through me. The low and narrow passage-way was squeezing me from side to side and top to bottom, and I twisted around to bolt back, then forced myself to stop, take a breath, blank my emotions, refuse to let panic rule me, turn back around, and continue to the end. Doug was behind me, and I feared that if I had to follow him out, unable to see past him and without breathing space, my panicked sense of confinement would multiply into flailing terror. The only way I could continue seeing in front of me was to keep moving forward—fast, because the faster I moved, the faster I would reach the end, and the faster I could turn around and get out of there.

Doug, about 10 feet behind me, suddenly sensed my panic, though I hadn't voiced it, and he called out, "They need an addi-tion to their sign that says, 'For the young, nimble, and one hun-dred pounders only.'"

I started giggling. At 125 pounds, I could barely shimmy through the narrow passageway without touching its sides, so at 60 pounds heavier, he was banging against those rock walls.

He added: "It's going to be pretty embarrassing if you have to go to the visitor's center for a crowbar to pry your husband loose."

I was still laughing when he warned: "Don't let them make you pay for it."

Right then, to my infinite relief, the end of the tunnel reared before us and widened into the "dungeon" where ole' Bob had periodically holed up to avoid detection by bears, Indians, and the law. It took me nearly a full second to appreciate Bob's old digs before I was whipping around to leave in half the time it took me to come in. I was scooting along that passageway like a Ninja Rabbit, and Doug was right on my heels.

The rest of our trek through that lovely gorge was accompanied by an array of sternly worded signs regarding appropriate conduct, written by someone who had lost all patience with ignorant and inconsiderate visitors. Signs such as "Positively No Picking of Flowers and Plants" were the dictates of a no-nonsense drill sergeant, although, "Don't Throw Things Over the Cliff Edge Onto the Trails Below" was an order that many visitors had diligently followed by tossing their soda cans and snack wrappers along the path. Since I have never discovered one good reason for littering this earth, especially its nature trails, I would have added the following addendum to that sign: "Or We Will Toss You into Bob's Old Dungeon and Disconnect the Lights."

The passageway leading to Bob's main hideaway—the cave where Bob spent most of his time in concealment—was a disheartening narrow channel which, from the first moment I gazed upon its entrance, began summoning forth another spell of claustrophobia. Yet even as I was paralyzed by the urge to never enter that corridor, I still wondered if I should force myself to "be brave" and "prove I could overcome" my claustrophobia.

While Doug and I were standing flat-footed, in mournful silence, and peering at that looming tunnel with funereal anticipation, two slender men in their late teens or early twenties unexpectedly appeared beside us and jauntily disappeared down that tunnel.

Doug finally voiced his aversion with this oblique comment: "I'm not so sure how smart Bob was. Which was worse, living in there or being in jail?"

I said, "Are you sure? I'll go if you want to."

He said, "You can go if you want, but I'm staying here, because that cave will look like all the other caves, and I don't feel like struggling to it," and armed with that satisfying justification for moving on, we did so without regret.

The morning we arrived, the gorge was, to our glee, mostly empty of people, but the afternoon brought the crowds, including a relentlessly obnoxious group—the kind that equates having fun with being loud, stupid, rude, selfish, thoughtless, and ill-mannered. Either they could not read or they lacked the intelligence to understand the huge signs they were having their pictures taken beside, because they immediately began screaming to produce an echo and throwing rocks over the cliffs onto the trails and the hikers below. We came upon them as they were debating which direction to go. I cheerfully advised them in my friendliest manner that there was an *extremely* interesting and *very* important cave that they *had* to see, and I pointed in the direction we had just come, which was opposite the direction we were going. I would have told them that Bob's lost gold had just been dug up had it sent them as far from us as possible.

They loped off, shouting and lobbing rocks, and we strolled the other way and enjoyed a peaceful examination of a series of small caves, situated high in the bank and sporting a narrow rock shelf along their forward edges that Doug described as "bear housing with front terraces."

A little later, heavy rocks began thudding on the trail just a few feet behind us, and the whooping and hollering from that obnoxious pack began blasting down on us from somewhere high above, echoing off the surrounding stone and physically hurting our ears. We could either leave or allow them to torment us with their audio clutter and ultimately ruin our day by bashing in our heads with the rocks they were enthusiastically heaving over the cliffs.

We exited the trail at a Wishing Well, made silent wishes to have fewer ignoramuses inhabiting this earth—or at least that was my wish—splurged by depositing a penny apiece, and watched a kid sacrifice a quarter, evidently not knowing, as Doug put it, that a quarter would not buy him any more at a Wishing Well.

Later that day, on our way to the small town of Hillsboro (the same Hillsboro where Johnny Paycheck engaged in the gun fight that landed him in jail), we stopped off at Paint Creek Lake, a reservoir, surrounded by a gigantic empty parking lot that easily could have stowed a fleet of 747s. A blinding sunlight poured onto and into that flat expanse of concrete and water to create an intense atmosphere of retained heat. A half dozen scattered trees offered no relief. Two men in a fishing boat, a pair of cyclists, and a couple perched at a picnic table, near a red convertible with its top down, were our only company. We turned our backs to the picnicking couple for maybe ten seconds maximum, turned around, and they had miraculously vanished. That barren landscape provided them with absolutely no place to go without being visible. Not even hunkering down on the seats or the floor of that red convertible would have concealed them. Had only one of us seen that couple, we would have suspected they were a hallucination, but we both saw them.

Where they disappeared to and how they managed it, we don't know, but we wished we had their talent so that we could return to Seven Caves and disappear those loud-mouths who had halfway ruined our visit. Instead, we disappeared ourselves by driving to the other side of the lake where a cluster of trees promised a meagre bit of shade and some respite from the glaring concrete. As we settled down to drink our pineapple juice, a pickup truck passed, hauling four heavyset, blondish and bearded guys in its bed, their heads lifted in the joyous pose of golden retrievers as the breeze ruffled their hair and beards. We waved, they waved.

Hillsboro welcomed us with a sharp and dangerous curve and a gleaming fluorescent orange sign too small for us to read until we were right on top of it. Doug opined that the sign warned that the county had lost people on that curve and didn't want to lose another, but up close, the sign carried only a disappointing message of support for the usual uninteresting political candidate. After browsing Hillsboro's antique shops, we ate dinner at the Wooden Spoon, whose menu was conclusive proof that nothing offered by a small-town restaurant would not ever be preceded by the word "fried." Their menu listed, as appetizers, "fried cheese stix, fried mushrooms, fried onion rings, fried potatoes, and a combination plate of all of the above."

Hillsboro taught us to never shop and have dinner before getting a motel room. We had confidently assumed that no one but the two of us would be trying to get a room in Hillsboro, Ohio, population about 6,500. Turns out, everyone was. By six in the evening, the town's only two decent motels were packed full. We cruised slowly past the other two—the shabby, single-story, strip kind where you park your car directly in front of your room's door, either to keep a suspicious eye on it or for a quick getaway when the cops show up. The first motel was an ancient, grungy building, particularly uninviting, and the second, even grubbier, had assembled four rough-hewn guys in the parking lot with the promising look of those who would wake us up at two a.m. to the sounds of them breaking beer bottles over each other's heads.

Fortunately, at no point throughout our entire trip were we ever more than two easy hours from Columbus or 30 minutes from an interstate—with all its glorious, neon lit, architecturally offensive truck stops, crammed elbow to elbow with up to 50 enticingly clean and trustworthy chain motels. We had sworn we wouldn't do it, but we sped off for the interstate at an admittedly eager velocity, absolutely lusting to once again see a six-lane highway and a hundred entrance ramps. I suggested the bed-and-breakfast we spotted on our way out of Hillsboro, but Doug said he wanted to spend the night in a bed that was longer than he was. He did not even slow down long enough for me to read their sign.

A mere 20 relieved minutes later, at the first exit off the interstate back toward Columbus, we were unpacking in a clean motel room inside a respectable building, without a single drunk biker monitoring the parking lot for victims.

Doug had gone in alone to rent our room, and he returned smiling: "That girl thought I was having an extramarital rendezvous."

I asked a baffled, "Why?"

"Well, I'm only 40 minutes from home (which she knew by the Columbus address he gave her), I'm wearing a ring, it's early in the evening, and I paid cash. I'm certain she thought I didn't want to leave a credit card trail for my wife to discover."

The best attribute of chain motel rooms that are clones of each other is that you always know what to expect. Not in that case. These people were ready to accommodate professional basketball players, for I have never seen a bathroom shower faucet positioned as high as that one. The bathroom ceiling was extra high to begin with, and the showerhead was up against the ceiling as if to get it out of reach of anyone who might try to steal it. The height dispersed the force of the water, prompting Doug to describe our showers as "like being caught in a light rain."

Still, we immensely enjoyed our extramarital rendezvous in a comfortable bed . . . up until midnight anyhow, for once again I did not sleep for the fourth night in a row. Knowing the trouble I was having, Doug had rented a room with two queen beds, and long about midnight, I transferred to the extra bed where I could more freely change position every two seconds in my futile attempt to force the energy to pass through my body instead of battering it. I had now tossed and turned through four nights and staggered through four days (heading into five) without genuine sleep. I was not sure how I was still standing.

**Sunday, Day 3: The Great Serpent Mound**

That next morning, we abandoned the interstate once again and continued southwest into an increasingly hilly landscape, almost storybook magical in its rolling hills and lovely valleys, though the beauty was not enticing enough for at least some of its inhabitants. While cruising through one flat little village we witnessed the most vivid verification possible of a place in which someone thinks there is absolutely nothing to do: a bored kid hugging a stop sign.

We were on our way to the Great Serpent Mound—if we could find it while using a map showing roads that did not exist, towns on roads the towns were not on, and roads that continued straight through towns, when in fact the roads completely dead-ended into other roads at right angles, forcing us to guess which of two opposing ways we should turn. The roads themselves were no help. Most of them lacked route signs, as if the locals knew where they were and no one else needed to know. I, as navigator, resorted to using the names of the towns we passed through to verify our course, reasoning that if the real-life towns we encountered on any road were in the same sequence as shown on the map (regardless of what road the map claimed the towns were on), then we were at least driving in the right direction.

Constantly guessing which road to take hindered our progress substantially, but without a compass to help us out, the position of the sun was an adequate substitute in keeping us on a road that headed in the general required direction, an approach that worked reasonably well until we came upon a bridge that was out, and, pun intended, things took a turn for the worse when it forced us into the second most unintelligent detour we have ever taken.

The first most unintelligent detour occurred years before on the west side of Columbus. That one led us on a 15-mile drive completely out of the city, into and past cornfields, and down a one-way road that dead-ended into a barricade. Our only exit was to retrace our route and go the wrong way on that one-way road.

During our second most unintelligent detour (on our way to the Great Serpent Mound), we faithfully and meticulously followed every single detour sign, and they unerringly took us right straight back to the brink of the bridge that was out.

Since neither of those two detours qualified as detours under any reasonable definition, we concluded that some bureaucrat in

Ohio's Transportation Department had hired the same people who had drawn our Rand McNally road map to draw the state's directions for detours.

Fortunately, Doug possesses an unmatched sense of direction that quickly found us a route around the broken bridge, across the stream, and into a village so tiny that it boasted only five buildings, one of which brazenly advertised itself as an antique shop. Junk shops pretending to a pedigree that will attract enough customers to stay in business inhabit every small town in America, but this was an actual antique shop, run by a talkative, tattoo-covered guy, though how he found more than one customer every six years in that isolated spot is a true wonder.

In noteworthy unexpectedness, Doug unearthed another piece of the crackle glassware he collects, and that pleasing little purchase enabled us to journey onward in a light mood only somewhat darkened by our increasing loss of faith in our map, and believe me when I say that our brand new, supposedly current map was at fault, not my skill at reading it. I'm a good navigator. For whatever reason, probably some old prior-life skill that I've carried over into this life, I can read a two-dimensional map (or floor plan) and relate it to my three-dimensional surroundings, although I've been reliably informed that many women cannot seem to get the hang of that.

The farther we travelled on those narrow hard-tack roads that corresponded with nothing on our map, the deeper we penetrated into an exceptionally pretty region of hilly farmland, whose beauty was our one compensation for having no clue where we were. At one point, when some guy out harvesting his field waved at us, Doug said uneasily: "Uh oh. We're in real trouble. You are *way* off the beaten trail when guys on tractors start waving because they haven't seen another life-form in a month."

Periodically, to ease our legitimate concern as to the ultimate end of some road we were on, we would pull off at one of the many small lakes we passed, spread a large beach towel beneath a shade tree, lean back, and drink some refreshing fruit juice to fortify our determination to plunge onward and persevere in our search for the Great Serpent Mound. The day was sunny and mild, the drive was slow and easy, the hilly farmland was pretty enough to attract hobbits from the Shire, and despite having to rely on some internal homing instinct—or maybe just haphazard luck—our course did finally lead us to the Great Serpent Mound, though we would have needed a satellite video of our journey to determine how we got there.

The Great Serpent Mound was different from other Indian Mounds I have been to. I grew up near a small village park that contained a small Mound, shaped like a chocolate drop, and back in the 1960s, every time our elementary school held a picnic there, we kids climbed the Mound and played all over it. That little Mound is still there—Doug and I visited it in 2020—and it has since acquired steps built into it that allow visitors to climb to its top, but it does not compare to the sheer uniqueness and mystery of the Great Serpent Mound.

The Serpent Mound was on a small bluff overlooking a creek and surrounded by well-kept land that contained an appealing visitor's center and picnic area. I did not know why I had come to the Serpent Mound—I have never been fascinated with the Indian Mounds, despite having grown up around them—but when we arrived, I knew this Mound was the spiritual center of our vacation. Although Ohio contains an abundance of Mounds, until this trip I knew almost nothing about them or their age, history, or purpose, except that they were supposedly burial grounds. I was also vaguely aware of the New Age claims about the Mounds, claims about "lost races" who supposedly built them, and claims about the "great energy" at the Serpent Mound. I had dismissed all those claims. I had always believed that any "great energy" at the Serpent Mound would be a primitive, elemental force from the Astral Plane, but certainly not from the Higher Mental or Divine Planes.

I do not wish to inadvertently add to the ignorant claims and general nonsense that surround the Great Serpent Mound, but I have to say that something unusual did happen to me at the Mound. Before walking the path that encircles the Mound, Doug and I went through the exhibit at the visitor's center in order to understand the Mound's history. We learned that the archaeologists, while extolling the Mound's beauty, symmetry, and perfect geometry, cannot say who built it or why it was built. They attribute it to the Adena culture, which they believe existed in Ohio between 1,000 BC and AD 500—as far back as 3,000 years ago—but beyond those general parameters, they do not know the exact age of the Serpent Mound. Excavations yielded no artifacts that enabled the archaeologists to date the Mound, give it a purpose, or determine why it was built. The archaeologists agree that the Great Serpent Mound was constructed for religious ceremonies and that it is not a burial Mound, although they have no artifacts or evidence to support either of those two conclusions or any other theories.

On the day of our visit, the weather was perfect, beautifully sunny and clear, warm but not hot. Fewer than a dozen people were present, so no one was with Doug and me at the top of the observation tower, and I was able to stand in silence, gaze down, view the entire Mound as a whole, and absorb the atmosphere.

I had to know: Was there a "great spiritual energy" at the Great Serpent Mound?

For four days, a tremendous flow of such energy had battered my body, and the last thing I needed was more of it. The Mound was beautiful, perfectly formed and peaceful, so very, very peaceful. No great energy emanated from it; it was just a mound of dirt, covered with grass, but as I gazed upon it, I realized the Mound was far more than its peaceful beauty because I knew why the Great Serpent Mound had been built. As this realization dawned in my consciousness, the ramifications off that understanding spread through my mind, and the relentless energy influx that had been tearing at my nervous system over the preceding week, unable to find balance, began to balance and align with the earth. A tremendous peacefulness and stillness pervaded my body, and I knew I was going to be able to sleep that night for the first time in days.

We descended the tower and circled the Mound counter-clockwise, halfway to the head, hiked the trail down to the creek at the bottom of the bluff, climbed back up to the tail end of the Mound, and circled it again, clockwise, completely, from tail to tail.

I will not tell you why the Great Serpent Mound was built. I will tell you only that I have stood at the center of Stonehenge, back on September 22, 1973, before it was closed to the general public, and I have stood at the Great Serpent Mound, and they were both built for the exact same reason. If you want to know "why" for yourself in regard to these ancient constructions, then ignore all those cockamamie ideas about lost races who built lost utopias, and aliens from other worlds that need landing pads for their spaceships, and just use your common sense and your intuitive insight, and sooner or later, you will arrive at the correct conclusion.

In late afternoon we reluctantly left the Great Serpent Mound's atmosphere of quiet peacefulness and travelled on to Portsmouth, an Ohio River town, and the closest town of a size that might offer a decent motel.

On the way, we entered the small village of Otway, and, upon noticing that the first three buildings we passed were churches, I commented: "This must be a very religious town."

The fourth building was a used clothing store with a sign announcing its name: "Born Again Clothing."

Doug replied: "Even their clothes are religious."

At a Ramada Inn in Portsmouth, for the first night in four nights, I slept, and I continued to sleep without energy interference every night for the remainder of our trip.

## Monday, Day 4: The Murphin Inn

Before we explored Portsmouth, Doug reluctantly agreed with my adventurous desire to eat breakfast at a local restaurant instead of seeking a routine meal at a familiar chain. We chose a place where I just knew I was going to be called "hon."

The restaurant's exterior was reasonably well maintained. On the inside, however, its warped, stained, and drooping ceiling tiles foretold that if anyone ever got ambitious enough to do some repair work, the results would definitely be noticed. A waitress in her forties, her hair sporting a brilliant, artificial shade of red, was sympathetically consoling an older gent at the counter that she fully understood how the wayward ways of his children would land them in jail because she had been down that path herself.

We were hungry, and hoping to get noticed by one of the kindhearted waitresses, we chose a table in the middle of the room, not far from a young woman and her beautiful little girl of not more than three years old. Shortly after we were seated, the woman grabbed a book and pretended to read in a futile effort to conceal her embarrassment that despite all her motherly admonishments, her little girl refused to stop staring and pointing at Doug, much to my amusement. I suspect the child was fascinated by his beard.

A waitress in her twenties delivered our coffee, set Doug's down, and started to place mine on the table when she exclaimed, "Why, hon! You got a floater in there!"

She marched away, either to remove the "floater" or get me a new cup.

Her lack of distress in regard to my "floater" indicated it was a common enough occurrence to merit a name, which alarmed me into throwing a panicked glance at Doug, who assured me that: "She probably just meant a coffee ground."

The coffee she brought back was hot enough to kill any "floaters" that still inhabited it. I drank it without asking her to define a "floater" and conceded to Doug that next time we wouldn't go local, at least not for breakfast.

We spent the day browsing the town's antique shops where

the last guy to ask, "Where you folks from?" told us about the murals painted on the river's flood wall. He was so puffed up proud that he made us promise to go see them. We went, not expecting much, but the artist had done a wonderful job.

When we left Portsmouth, we drove northwest into gentle, rolling hills dotted with patches of Amish farms that alternated with tracts of forest, all of it enhanced by a serene atmosphere and a lot of hearses. The locals had decided it was a good day for burying their friends and relatives, for during that short drive, we joined one funeral procession and passed three cemeteries conducting funerals.

Late that afternoon after navigating a tangled maze of backroads that curled in and through and around Amish farms, we finally located and checked in at our second B&B. I had specifically requested and reserved one of their two rooms that offered a queen size bed, but I still spent that entire drive, from Portsmouth to the Inn, ceaselessly reassuring an anxious Doug, right up to the moment he physically lay down on that queen bed, that he would be able to fit inside it.

The friendly owners of the Murphin Ridge Inn, which was just a little south of the Great Serpent Mound, had transformed the downstairs of the original house, built in the 1820s, into a restaurant, and the upstairs into an art gallery for displaying local artists. They lived in another newer house on the property, and guests were quartered in a Shaker-style guest house near an outdoor pool and croquet court.

After settling into our fastidiously clean room—not a dust mote hanging anywhere—we walked a flat, short trail through the woods, then showered, and in their lovely dining room, we tucked into a most satisfying gourmet dinner, cooked by the female half of the owners. I invited their only other guest, a female Christian minister on a personal retreat, to sit with us for dinner so that the three of us could exchange our small talk in a more sensible and less ridiculous manner than shouting at each other across the room.

We followed that most agreeable dinner and conversation with a tour of the upstairs art room, then relaxed outside in the chilly air on comfortable chairs positioned on a concrete patio that surrounded a fire, built within a pit dug into the ground. In late evening, the rest of the group departed. I shifted onto Doug's lap, the Murphin Inn's cat climbed onto my lap, and the three of us spent the next hour staring blissfully up at the Milky Way—a vivid band of mist and stars, spread across the sky.

We deeply regretted not scheduling two nights there.

Sherry, the female owner, had earlier told us that the Cincinnati Astronomical Society held their meetings at the Inn because the ridge offered such an expansive view of the sky. After learning we had come from the Great Serpent Mound, she said they received a lot of Serpent Mound customers, and two women stayed a couple of times per year in order to visit the Mound and "refuel their crystals." The women had told Sherry that they see a vast array of colors at the Mound. I told her only that I had experienced a great peacefulness.

Breakfast at the Murphin Inn was as gourmet as dinner had been and just as abundant. My small taste of Doug's French toast stuffed with a cream cheese and fruit mixture was sensational, but I opted for oatmeal to reduce the high fat, high sugar "road diet" I was being forced to eat that was killing my body. Since I was not getting the exercise I needed and was accustomed to (which increases my oxygen intake, which increases my metabolism, which helps my body process the small amount of fat I do intake), the oatmeal was the preferred choice—and a good choice, the best oatmeal I have ever had. Sherry said she got it from Canada.

Immediately after breakfast, we packed the truck for our departure but chose to delay leaving in order to hike the long, hilly trail on the other side of their 141 acres. The hike was supposed to take an hour, maybe 90 minutes, and it would have, but a slight error in judgment on our part cost us three hours. Where our brains departed to that morning when we left the trail, I cannot say, because we are *always* obedient to the signs that emphatically warn hikers not to leave the trails. We never go off them because we know it's easy to get lost, and we know that thousands of people routinely galloping off the trails and trashing through the woods will destroy the landscape. Neither of us was able to recall, from the moment we did it, why we thought abandoning the trail was a good idea, probably because, to recall the facts would lay one of us open to being responsible for the idea and the other to agreeing to it, and neither of us was willing to do either.

It happened this way: The branch of the trail we were on dead-ended at a creek. Instead of smartly turning around and retreating along that same trail to our starting point, we chose to "take a shortcut" and hike up the partially dried creek bed to a previous point where we had seen the creek intersect the main trail we were on. Neither of us was willing later on to take credit for generating this superb idea, although neither of us went so far as to blame the other either. Despite neither of us producing or supporting this idea, we proceeded to carry it out by entering and hiking the halfway dried-up creek bed, studded with scattered stones, bordered by cliffs, and interspersed with waterfalls that we were forced to scale—short ones and not fully gushing due to a recent drought, but waterfalls all the same.

At the first waterfall, Doug suggested we turn around, but I was determined: "No, no, we've come this far, we go on."

So, we went on . . . and on . . . and on . . . and we were *not* coming to the intersection where the main trail curved in and met the stream, although we knew it did because we had crossed that very spot while traveling the main trail. After two hours of slushing through that stream bed, searching for some sign of the main trail, it dawned on us like a spiritual revelation from a mountaintop that the stream was taking its time to wander back to where it met the trail because the stream curled like a complex pretzel all around and behind and up and down and in and through those rocky, tree-covered hills.

Although both of us had grown up in the country (and I had grown up in very hilly country, cut every which way by creeks and small rivers), and we were both fully educated in the devious, curly, winding nature of streams, we had failed to recall—at the precise moment when we really needed it—the wisdom we had gleaned from our childhood environments.

Instead, we just trudged on, while Doug kept getting increasingly nervous and periodically tried to get my attention by wondering out loud if we were lost, and I insisted on marching resolutely forward, knowing the creek had to wind back to that junction with the trail. Besides, we had already hiked so far that any retreat would triple the time devoted to our "shortcut." He acquiesced, partly because he knew I was right and partly because he enjoyed photographing the stream from its reverse side.

Getting lost did not actually worry me. What worried me were the rocks we were using as stepping stones to avoid wading. Rocks inside or edging stream beds are notoriously unstable. I feared stepping on one and having it tip and dump a nest of water moccasins onto my feet, at least three of which would be angry enough to sink their fangs into my ankles and pitch me face-first into that drought-stricken creek's shallow mixture of mud and water.

As the sun climbed higher and it seemed increasingly likely that we would find our way out just in time for dinner, the stream's junction with the main trail mercifully appeared and we gratefully hiked its long length back to the Inn. When we finally staggered from the woods, our sweaty, trembling bodies and wet trousers blotched with mud up to our knees were blatant evidence of our reckless disregard of their stern trail rules. So, we just waved good-bye from a distance, beat it to our vehicle, revved the engine, and pulled away before our hosts could get a close look at us.

We wanted to let the innkeepers know they should cut another trail to a truly beautiful set of cliffs and waterfalls we had seen, but we couldn't think of a way to conceal how we found them. We doubted we could elicit their smiling approval by saying (even in a tone of bighearted helpfulness): "Hey . . . if you leave the trail and hike up the stream bed about two miles . . ."

## Tuesday, Day 5: A Night By The River

**Georgetown:** Our stopover in Georgetown, the boyhood home of Ulysses S. Grant and currently inhabited by about 4,500 residents, was intended to be a quick side trip, a precursor to Ripley, a little town perched right on the edge of the Ohio River, where we were scheduled to stay in the B&B that Grant had boarded at as a student.

However, finding Georgetown was like engaging in a particularly difficult scavenger hunt, as our map did not reflect even one of the roads we travelled or towns we passed through on our way to Georgetown. The map's roads either did not exist in the real world, or other roads by other names existed in their places. Just as frustrating was how the map size of the towns did not correspond with their actual earthly size. The map often indicated that a "town," which in real life was two ramshackle houses, facing off across a dusty one-lane trail, was the same size or even bigger than a booming burg of 20,000, featuring an industrious town square, an official courthouse, and a big brick elementary school named after some president. This disparity interfered in our well-laid plans for obtaining gas, food, and ice for our cooler to keep our fruit juice cold. After too many disappointments that gradually reduced our food, fuel and ice to an alarmingly low level, a bleak intersection featuring a rundown gas station and an outdoor vending machine that had been kicked way too many times—and still wouldn't dispense anything—was cause for an impromptu celebration.

Non-existent route signs were another problem. Either some Highway Department's stuffed shirt had nixed route signs from the road budget, or else thieves regarded the signs as highly desirable souvenirs, because we often traveled miles and crossed dozens of intersecting roads without finding a single route sign, and we needed at least one to determine if anything on our map was within a 50-mile radius of where we were.

At one point, the road we were on, which, supposedly, would lead directly west into Georgetown, dead-ended into a road running north and south and did not continue west for the next 30 miles as the map emphatically proclaimed via the boldest of its lines. As official navigator, I was forced to tell the pilot, Doug, that it was now his turn to take a guess as to where we were. Since none of the villages we had passed through corresponded with anything on our map, all I could say for certain was that we were facing into the descending sun, which meant we were facing west; therefore, if we turned right, we would eventually reach Lake Erie on Ohio's northern border, and if we turned left, we would eventually reach the Ohio River on the state's southern border. South was the direction we had to go in order to be in Ripley by that evening to make use of our B&B reservation. So, we turned south onto a semi-decent road of tarred gravel.

About a quarter of a mile later, we passed a UPS driver, parked alongside the road and studying a map. I was badly tempted to holler out the window: "If your map is Rand McNally, you'll wander these roads for days."

Doug just said with weary patience: "Now we have two clues for knowing when we're lost in nowhere—people on tractors waving at us and a UPS driver studying a map."

How I finally navigated us to Georgetown is a secret I would be unable to reveal under any form of torture, because the truth is, we simply stumbled across it. We travelled so many roads looking for it that we eventually found ourselves on the only road we had not yet been on, and it held Georgetown.

The Grant house was closed, so, disappointed but now accustomed to the way all the small-town museums opened only if they had visitors, we strolled up the street a short distance to the first building that contained a business (an art shop) and inquired how we could enter the Grant house/museum. Within seconds, what we thought would be a quick 15-minute stop transformed into a nearly three-hour stop, all because we had fortuitously chanced upon a wonderful Kentucky woman by the name of Lee, who was not only the director of the art gallery, but also the curator of the Grant house/museum.

Lee was a captivating riot. She was tall, slender, and attractive. Her blonde hair was rolled into a twist, and she was dressed quite tastefully in an off-white linen suit, elegantly complemented by a grey blouse and grey shoes featuring four-inch spike heels. Lee proceeded to escort us back to the Grant house which, in this hilly little town, was literally downhill from her gallery. She was barely able to walk on the cobblestone sidewalk in her four-inch spike heels, so we slowed our pace to match hers, which brought all three of us nearly to a standstill. After several attempted steps she abandoned the sidewalk for the smoother surface of the street, and 10 minutes later we had all managed to travel the 30 feet to the little museum.

Lee put us through a nearly three-hour lecture tour of this small house, including all the gossip about the Grant family, their relatives, friends, and acquaintances, while punctuating it all with flamboyant gestures and speech. Although she could barely climb up and down the stairs in her shoes, she was a genuine entertainer who transformed a dry, boring visit to an unremarkable little house into a memorable history lesson.

As Doug said later, "She loved gossip and talking and it made her perfect for what she does."

She was thrown off her stride only once—when she started to say, "My hometown is . . ." and I finished for her, "in Kentucky." But she didn't know that after spending four years in the military, listening to accents from every region of the United States, I became extremely good at distinguishing the accents peculiar to the many different southern states. Too many people lump southern accents together, usually giving them all an Appalachian *Beverly Hillbillies* quality, but they are not one big indistinguishable lump. The accents of Tennessee, Georgia, Texas, the Carolinas are all different. The southern Ohio accent, while unlike the central or northern Ohio accent and more alike to a southern or Dixie accent, is still not the same as the West Virginia or Kentucky accent, despite the slimmest border separating the states, and though Lee was living in southern Ohio, the nuances in her accent were Kentucky.

After concluding our tour with cheery goodbyes, we started toward our car and Lee began laboring back up the hill when she had second thoughts about a bit of gossip she had divulged, and she turned and called out a request for us not to repeat what she had told us. We promised we wouldn't.

Once inside the privacy of our truck, Doug, grinning, said, "She needs to ditch those shoes."

I said, "Oh, no, she can't! It would ruin her. The shoes are perfect, just the right final touch."

He said: "You're right. She has to keep the shoes."

From Lee we learned that Grant, whose pictures portray him as the stodgiest of old guys, was actually quite a roustabout, loved to travel, couldn't keep a job due to his lack of sustained interest in anything, found out he was going to West Point when he arrived home one day to the startling news that his father had surreptitiously signed him up for it, and is believed to be our first celebrity endorser as he was paid a fee for lending his name and face to the sale of products after his presidency.

My favorite fact: His name wasn't really Ulysses S. Grant. It was actually Hiram Ulysses Grant, but when he went to West Point at age 17, he deliberately reversed his first two names to avoid having the initials H.U.G. on his luggage and prevent being teased by fellow cadets. He became U.H.G. In the meantime, he received some additional interference on the issue of his name that can only be classified as Divine. The official who processed his paperwork put his name down as Ulysses Simpson Grant (Simpson was his mother's maiden name), and Ulysses, quite rightly seeing a good thing on his horizon—that being the golden opportunity to say a grateful goodbye to Hiram forever—never bothered to correct the error. Henceforth he went down in history as Ulysses S. Grant.

During the course of our tour, Lee asked where we were going, and we told her to Ripley to the house Grant had boarded at as a student. We had stopped in Georgetown first to get his background information. She informed us that the owner of the Ripley B&B had been taken to the hospital over the weekend with a life-threatening spinal condition related to her eyes.

**Ripley:** We drove on to Ripley, expecting to sleep in the bed of our truck that evening and possibly attend a funeral the next day, but at the Grant Cottage, a note attached to the door advised us to walk up the street about three house numbers to another B&B, the Signal House.

Back in June, when I had planned our vacation, I had initially called the Signal House because it had been part of the Underground Railroad, but the owner, after saying they would be doing house repair work that week, had referred me to her friend up the street who operated the Grant Cottage.

At the Signal House we learned that the Grant Cottage owner was still in the hospital but out of danger, and the Signal House owner was taking us in to give us a place to stay. We expressed our profuse gratitude. They gave us our choice of two beautiful upstairs rooms, and we chose the one that overlooked the Ohio River. Since the Signal House was literally on the river's edge—separated from the river only by a space the width of the two-lane street that ran between the house and the river—our second-floor room gave us a wonderful, comprehensive view.

They showed us their lovely home first. Although we couldn't tell it, a flood only two years before in 1997 had forced them to redo carpeting and wallpaper after getting nine inches of water in the house. Yet that deluge was still better than the 1937 flood when the river water had reached the second floor. We were amazed the house had even survived. Doug asked me later, privately, how people could tolerate the destructive flooding, but I told him that it comes with the river. Having grown up beside it, I would not voluntarily live against it and have to deal with the floods, but I understand the mindset of the people. The river is mesmerizing; it pulls you in and holds you. Even now, 60 years later, I retain a clear memory image of the barges, loaded with coal, floating silently down the river at night while the beauty of their lights reflected and danced in the water like fairy creatures.

Ripley had no restaurant, but the innkeepers helpfully fanned out an array of about a dozen menus from restaurants within a 15-mile radius. Cost was all we had to rely on to ascertain quality, so we selected one of their three highest-priced restaurants whose entrées ran between twelve dollars and sixteen dollars, not high in a big city, but high for that region in that year. Our hosts confirmed the food was well prepared and provided us with directions—up the river about 10 miles and across the bridge into Kentucky to a little town called Maysville. It was here on the menu of this large and busy restaurant that I found the regional favorite of fried frog legs. I informed Doug in the superior and knowledgeable tone of a highbrow food critic that "with rice and vegetables" was not how frog legs should be eaten. They should be eaten the way my brother Randy and I ate them as a child—with unripe gooseberries and green onions we pulled from the garden and washed off in the creek.

We were ordering an inexpensive wine from Kathy, our waitress, when she popped the same question we had already heard several times, "Where you folks from?"

I laughed and asked, "Is it that obvious?"

She tried to brush it off, but later, when we left, she called after us: "Now you have a good trip."

The various restaurants we had eaten at throughout our trip had plied us with truckloads of food, and I knew that if the portions were large I could never eat an entrée, plus the bowl of soup I yearned for, plus the salad I desperately needed. When I explained my dilemma, Kathy cocked her head sideways to examine the size of my body under the table, straightened, and said, "Ahh, hon, you don't want that soup. All that water will just bloat you up."

Kathy had wisely warned me away from the soup, because the portions of our meal were sizable and good enough that we stuffed ourselves before returning to Ripley.

The owners of the Signal House, unlike those at a lot of B&Bs, lived in their home and slept in the upstairs bedroom across from the guest room that we occupied. Thus we were literal guests in their home, which produced a far different atmosphere from the two preceding B&Bs, especially the one in Chillicothe. (One important and gratifying difference is that when the owners live in the B&B, it tends to be clean and clutter free.) However, until we returned from dinner at about ten p.m. and found them in bed with their bedroom door closed, I had not quite realized that they slept upstairs in the room across from ours. Had I known that, I would have taken some precautions before we left for dinner.

For starters, I would have announced loudly that I rise at least once during the night, sometimes twice, to use the toilet and dispense the quarts of water that I drink throughout the day— which I keep drinking every time I wake during the night. They, however, had failed to warn us that the door to our bedroom, when opened, would not stay put, but would instead, instantly swing all the way back, clunk up against a small chest behind the door, bounce off and hurtle shut with a resounding thud.

So, Doug and I returned that late evening to a quiet house, our hosts asleep in their room, opposite ours, and we went upstairs and onto the adjoining balcony overlooking the river—about 30 feet away—and sat for a few minutes in the night air before showering and bedding down in a beautiful, clean, non-dusty room, with me forgetting three important things: The water jug in our truck, containing purified water, free of all chlorine, the train track that runs down the West Virginia, Kentucky side of the Ohio River, and the kind of noise that comes off the river, a noise I had not heard since I was 16 and living in a house on the edge of a park that adjoined an Ohio River lock and dam. Although barges and boats can float down the Ohio in utter silence, they can also make a lot of racket. When you live beside those sounds, you get accustomed to them, and during my teens, I actually liked them. I was especially partial to the rumble and whistle of the train on the opposite side of the river. That, however, was my life 30 years before this trip. My ears were no longer adapted to the sounds.

About two-thirty a.m., a whistle blasted directly in my ear; then a second one blew, followed by a massive amount of rumbling and clanging and booming, and I jerked straight up in bed, my entire body jittering, having no idea where I was or what was happening. The train across the river was thundering by and announcing its presence, which happened to coincide with three boats going up the river in succession, a tugboat, a steamship, and a barge, all of them tooting and rooting at each other in a hearty exchange of riverboat hellos out on the water.

As I jerked upright in bed, Doug also woke, and, as is his habit in such moments, he reared up and screamed my name. He does this because his first concern is where I am and what is happening to me, but yelling my name increases my confusion and panic because I don't know if he's screaming for help or screaming to help me.

With Doug hollering my name, and both of us only half awake and thus half aware, and all that yet to be defined noise out on the river only about 30 feet from our ears, we were thrashing and struggling with confining bedcovers as if they were enemy combatants, all the while trying to determine where we were and who we were fighting. Somewhere in this chaos, enough childhood memories filtered up to my conscious awareness that I was finally able to mumble, "It's the river boats, it's the river boats," and Doug, satisfied that I had the danger under control, dropped back down.

In that moment of calmness, I came just far enough awake to realize that I badly needed to use the toilet and that my distracting physical discomfort was contributing to my addled mental state. So, to solve both problems, I hopped out of bed to visit the bathroom, but the bed was much higher than ours at home, and being unaccustomed to the greater distance, I incorrectly timed my landing, hit the floor off balance, and crumpled sideways, gasping and groaning and clutching at the edge of the bed in an effort to haul myself erect, which brought Doug bolting upright once again, hollering, "Huh? You okay? What's happening?"

My assurances that it was just me, going to the bathroom, settled him, and I proceeded to the door and the hallway leading to the bathroom at its other end, absolutely certain that our hosts were lying wide awake, staring regretfully at the ceiling, and wishing to God they had told us to drive to Cincinnati if we wanted a place to sleep for the night.

Now, this house was built in the 1830s, which made it, at the time of our stay, about 170 years old. The bedroom door would not stay put when it was only partway open, and it didn't latch thoroughly either. I was still half asleep, and when I opened the door, then shut it behind me, I thought I had pulled it so that it latched and would not swing back, but I hadn't, and it swung back, way back and way too fast, clunked the corner of the chest behind it and hurtled off. Doug reared up again, screaming my name, and I, out in the hallway now, turned around to stumble back and apologize and maybe cut the noise down a little.

Returning to the room was not so easy, however, because the hallway was severely warped, something else I had forgotten. Although the house was well taken care of and well decorated with beautiful wallpaper, carpeting and furnishings, the 170 years and previous flooding to the second floor had taken their toll on the structure itself. The hallway floor slanted away from the wall in a gradual tilt toward the balustrade of the balcony-styled hallway that encircled the stairwell. I had noticed this sloped floor when we checked in and, fully alert and in daylight, I had automatically accommodated my step to it. Now, half asleep and in the dark with the warp forgotten, I didn't know where to put my feet to stand up straight enough to walk, and I navigated that sloped hallway like a drunk reeling from wall to railing and back again.

After staggering back to the bedroom and closing the door properly to keep it from repeatedly swinging and banging, I slowly traversed the hall to the bathroom, used it, and carefully made my way back to the bedroom, where I drank the water in the glass I had filled and left on the nightstand prior to going to bed. (I leave water by my bed even at home to avoid getting out of bed during the night to forage for it.) Unfortunately, I had used their tap water, not our filtered water, which was still in the truck, and their water was heavily chlorinated. Chlorinated water instantly bleaches my throat and mouth bone dry, but since it was all I had, I drank it and dropped off to sleep.

About four a.m. another rooting and tooting session out on the river woke me to a throat and mouth so parched from chlorine I could barely breathe. I desperately needed water.

Somewhere in the dim memory banks of my sleep-deprived brain, I recalled our hostess indicating a tray of glasses and a bottle of water for our personal usage. The problem now was locating it, quietly, as our hosts were sleeping in the room opposite ours, and our two doors were separated only by about six feet, which was the length of the front balcony that led off that upstairs hallway.

Once again, I hopped out of bed and failed to remember the greater height, hit the floor off balance, clutched at the nearby table, missed it, and fell up against the wall before bouncing off and hitting a dresser, all the time grunting and groaning and fighting off furniture in my grim determination to stay upright. Eventually I blundered to the exit, where I again failed to latch the door, which swung rapidly and hit the corner of the chest with another loud clunk, causing Doug to jackknife upright and scream my name for the fourth time that night.

I called to Doug in a conspicuously loud stage whisper that it was just me, seeking water, although, speaking frankly, it wouldn't have mattered if I had yelled it. I expected my hostess to emerge from her bedroom at any minute, tying on a robe, and saying: "Hon, why don't I put on some coffee and start breakfast and we'll just call it a night. Hmm?"

Out on the slanted hallway floor, I staggered along it alternately clutching the railing on one side and the wall on the other, and found the water only when I missed the railing and seized a table for support, and there was the water, sloshing invitingly in its container. So, I snapped to and poured and downed glass after glass of water, grateful for our hostess's foresight, but wishing to God I had brought in my own. No matter how much chlorinated water I drink, I remain thirsty. Many people complain that water does not quench their thirst, but the chlorine is the reason, because nothing quenches thirst like natural spring or well water.

As badly as I wanted my own water, I did not dare leave the house, despite our vehicle being parked right outside their front door. God knows what they would have thought I was up to had I gone blundering through their home, knocking over furniture, clearing tables, slamming up against the walls, and rattling unfamiliar door handles.

I drank until I was full and returned to bed, terribly embarrassed over all the noise, especially because they had been gracious enough to take us in during their vacation. They could have told us, "Sorry. Drive over to Maysville. You'll be eating there anyhow." Or they could have sent us to the third B&B in town which was not nearly as nice as theirs, at least not from the outside.

When we rose that morning, the river was beautiful, half covered with fog, and from our view off the balcony, I told Doug, "This is why the river gets inside you."

He understood and wanted to return in the future and give the Ohio more time.

I said: "If they'll ever rent a room to us again."

At breakfast, our hostess asked if we had heard the Delta Queen go by during the night. I assumed that was her tactful way of giving me an opening to confess the night's shenanigans in the hope of determining just exactly what I had been up to. I admitted to hearing something and added that I hoped I had not disturbed her by clanking the door and all the other noise I had made while going to the bathroom and searching for water.

She said oh no, I hadn't disturbed her; she was often up in the night, and she had been restless and risen and wandered around the house and sent some email.

For someone who hadn't been disturbed she had certainly been active, but it seemed best to drop the subject while we were all still being polite about it.

Actually, our hosts were agreeably friendly, and during our long breakfast chat, Doug offered some advice as to what was in keeping with the repairs and upkeep on a historic house such as theirs. After which, they were so talkative and comfortable that we could barely break away, though in the midst of that, she told me one important thing.

When I mentioned that the author of our guidebook could not possibly have stayed in the Chillicothe B&B where we had spent our first night, she told us with an exasperated expression of "Can you believe it?" that the author had never once stayed at their B&B either, despite his glowing review—which confirmed my certainty that he had gathered his information from advertising brochures or telephone interviews or by plagiarizing someone else's guidebook.

## Wednesday, Day 6: The Reverend Rankin

After breakfast at the Signal House, we explored the ancient houses that lined Ripley's historic district, and just for the pleasure of eating in an old-time soda shop called the "Rockin' Robin," I ordered a hot fudge sundae that I did not need. A wall display of pictures showed the shop's crew with newswoman Barbara Walters, athlete O.J. Simpson's lawyer, and actor Steven Seagal. What brought those three to Ripley to eat sundaes in the Rockin' Robin Soda Shoppe was a mystery, but the pictures proved they had been there, and seemingly all at the same time, because the Shoppe's personnel were wearing the same clothes in all three pictures. I could not imagine that any of those celebrities had even heard of Ripley, unless they were researching Ohio River floods or the Underground Railroad.

The Rockin' Robin's counter girl informed us proudly that during the last major flood, the water got up halfway in their shop and left "a ton of yucky stuff" and "everything had to be disinfected and redone."

We resumed our stroll along the length of Ripley's historic district, which lines the river's edge just inches away from every flood that courses through. Most of their historic district was part of the Underground Railroad, prior to the Civil War. In fact, Ripley was the seat of the most extreme abolitionist activity in the Ohio River Valley, due primarily to a single-minded character called the Reverend John Rankin.

The Reverend Rankin was a Presbyterian preacher who, according to his autobiography, which I bought and read, hated "profane language," the "use of spirits," "frolicking and dancing," and human slavery. (Privately, I think the Reverend didn't have as much against "frolicking" as he claimed, because he produced 13 children.) I doubt seriously that the Reverend knew the meaning of the word "compromise," because he devoted his entire life to the preaching of the gospel as it centered on what he regarded as the most important of the Biblical statements—that all human beings were created equal in the eyes of God. That scripture propelled him relentlessly into the abolition of slavery starting somewhere around 1815. In the Reverend's autobiography, he said he voluntarily left Kentucky because it wasn't receptive to his preaching against slavery. Other sources say he was run out of Kentucky for preaching against slavery and teaching slaves to read, but whichever version is accurate, and most likely both are, he settled in Ripley, just across the Ohio River from Kentucky, where he began to offer his home as a safe house for the fugitive slaves who were smuggled across the river.

Part of his home still stands on a hill, high above Ripley, and it's now a small, but history-saturated museum, as is the hill itself, nicknamed "Liberty Hill." From its top, visitors can take in a comprehensive view of the valley, the town, and the Ohio, and easily imagine the tense evenings that the Reverend stood watch over all movement down below in his unwavering determination to complete his obligation to God and humanity. The Signal House was part of the network of houses along the river that placed lanterns in the skylights of their roofs to signal Rankin up on the hill with an "all clear" sign—(that the river was clear of bounty hunters, slave catchers, bloodhounds)—and that the Rankins were free to move their fugitives.

I also bought and read John Parker's autobiography, another prominent antislavery person who worked with Rankin. Parker was an ex-slave, although the book's promotional information said only that he was a prominent citizen who had owned and operated a foundry, he had lived in one of the large houses by the river, and his children had all been college graduates. I read his fascinating story straight through, unable to put it down. Parker's autobiography contained a telling statement—that the real story and truth of the abolitionists would never be told because their real activity, everything that went on behind the scenes that was illegal by the laws of the land, had to be kept secret for their safety. Since the truth could not be revealed, those who knew the real story would all die and take with them the truth of what they had done and how they had done it.

A good example was the incident that became *Uncle Tom's Cabin*, which was based on a real event told by Reverend John Rankin to Harriet Beecher Stowe, but she could not credit him (or the real "Eliza" who crossed the river on the ice) because to do so was to provide the evidence and testimony that would endanger the lives of the abolitionists and expose their Underground network.

Because so many of the old houses still stand, and because so many of them are well taken care of (despite the periodic determination of the Ohio River to drown them), the town of Ripley does not give the impression that you've entered a theme park (which happens when towns restore their historic areas). The Ripley of today retains a general sense of what it was like 150 years ago, and with the history that pervades the town's physical forms also pervading the very atmosphere, it was difficult not to feel ourselves slipping quietly back in time in response to the subtle impact on our psyche.

We left Ripley and headed downriver toward Cincinnati to become the only visitors at the Captain Anthony Meldahl Lock and Dam. The glaring sun was unpleasantly hot on top of the barren lock, but our luck held otherwise, because a barge was floating downriver, and Doug had never seen a barge go through a lock, had never seen the water raised and released. We passed the time waiting for the barge by betting how long it would take to reach us. He said 15 minutes. I said 30. We claimed we both won when it got there in 22 minutes (midway), and we each defended our claim with the flimsy excuse that we had not clearly defined, prior to the bet, whether "reaching us" meant one end of the barge touching the tip of the lock or the length of the barge being inside it.

We lingered, watching a small boat called the *Leading Lady* float pertly through one lock and the *John M. Rivers* barge lumber mightily through the other, and we felt hot and happy and content with life until a group of loud-voiced women arrived. For some unfathomable reason, too many people nowadays think it's necessary to blight the atmosphere of all public places with raucous noise to ensure the attention of everyone present is riveted on them. Their booming discussion about their excited desire to witness a barge traverse a lock, which they had never seen, automatically included anyone within 100 feet. So, since another barge was already floating with slow, determined intention toward the lock, I joined their conversation by telling them to wait a few minutes and they would be rewarded with what they had come to see.

I knew they would not wait. Five minutes of quiet patience was as alien to them as manners.

Within a minute of that group's arrival, Doug and I gladly abandoned them and their unnecessary racket to visit Grant's birthplace in Point Pleasant (different from his boyhood home of Georgetown where he grew up, and Ripley where he boarded). As we pulled into the parking lot beside his birthplace home, the women from the lock commandeered the space right beside us, once again contaminating the air with their boisterous chatter.

As expected, they had not bothered to wait for the barge. They thumped and clunked and loudmouthed their way through the Grant house, disturbing the atmosphere so much that we couldn't enjoy it, quite a contrast with our experience in Georgetown and with the entire town of Ripley.

They were from Cincinnati and they were using the day to tour historical sites along the Ohio. They left the Grant house even before we did, bragging to each other as they loaded into their car that they had now "seen that one too" and could "check it off their list of things to visit." I could have told them that they would enjoy the sites more if they would take the time to experience them and not just look at them, but I stayed silent. I have a dislike of being stared at with blank, uncomprehending eyes.

**Thursday, Day 7: Lebanon and Waynesville**

Lebanon and its nearby neighbor, Waynesville, are major antique places in Ohio, and that Thursday, after leaving Point Pleasant and arriving in Lebanon, we had their nearly empty-of-customers antique stores to ourselves in contrast to the huge Saturday crowds that we had encountered many years before when we had quickly stopped in Lebanon on our way back from Cincinnati and just as quickly left, unable to penetrate the hordes of shoppers. This time we had the open space needed to amble through their many stores in search of a unique soap dish for use in our art studio. Nothing was available in the exact color and shape we sought, and the prices on the ones that almost worked ranged up to fifty dollars. Call us stingy, but fifty dollars for a soap dish that stood a 90 percent chance of getting broken was an unnecessary expenditure, although had it been truly beautiful, perfect, and of some historic value, we would have sprung for it. We also would have set it on a shelf and never used it.

By the time we finished in Lebanon and reached Waynesville, we were antiqued out. So, in Waynesville, we opted to visit a museum, a visit that was aborted by a handwritten, unsigned, unaddressed note hanging on its locked door that said: "Ladies, when you arrive, please come to my office, and I'll let you in."

Without a name, an address, an office, or any of the ladies we could tag along with, we shrugged off Waynesville, drove to the outskirts of Dayton, and signed up for two nights at a Holiday Inn that offered a pool and a hot tub where Doug could ease his neck, which was still painfully stiff from sleeping in that too short, antique bed back in Chillicothe.

All the rooms at the Holiday Inn had been positioned in a circle around the motel's pool and its related activities/recreation area, and the balconies off the rooms overlooked this space. Doug was eagerly anticipating a session in the pool and the hot tub, but because it was near bedtime and we were hungry, we opted for dinner instead at an adjoining restaurant. The Inn was blessedly quiet, and on the way through the hallways and lobby to the restaurant, we passed five security people, pacing the building with little walkie-talkie communicators and exuding the confident air of being in command of our safety.

## Friday, Day 8: Dayton

The next morning, our door would not lock, and because we were staying another night and leaving our belongings in our room, we delayed our departure while we tracked down the manager and ensured our door was repaired. We skipped breakfast, being stuffed from our late meal the previous evening.

Our first stop was the Dayton Art Institute and its special exhibit of the work of Norman Lewis, an abstract expressionist that neither of us had ever heard of. The pamphlet said he was African American and the exhibit was part of some Harlem promotion of overlooked artists who were victims of racism. Politically motivated exhibits rarely offer anything but mediocre to bad work that is being falsely promoted as great in order to justify and gratify someone's desire to screech about racism or sexism. Consequently, we were not expecting anything of value when we wandered into this exhibit, but to our complete surprise, we were suddenly standing in the midst of the work of the best abstract expressionist who was painting during the period that style was born. The real horror though, the real racism, was that he was *still* being judged by his skin color, not his talent, by being categorized as an "African American" artist and not just simply as an artist, the best of his era and style.

Against our better judgment, we opted for lunch at the museum, knowing that any time you eat lunch at an art museum, you're making a donation to the museum, because the standard museum food portion is one level tablespoon of something pretentious and excessively expensive. (One time in hungry desperation in Washington DC, we paid nearly ten dollars apiece for teensy, dried out cucumber sandwiches—about one small bite.) Before I ordered every selection on the entire Dayton Art Institute's menu—the salad, soup, a sandwich, a fruit plate and dessert to take the edge off my hunger before afterwards picking up two fish sandwiches and an extra large fry at a fast-food place—I interrogated the waitress about portion sizes. She said they were substantial. I did not honestly believe her, but to our astonishment, the platters needed crimped edges to contain the overflow. Fortunately, I had held off and not ordered the fruit plate and dessert, for I could barely cram down what she brought me. Three women at a nearby table requested one slice of chocolate cake for dessert and split it—and even that was making an overeating demand on their stomachs. Their gigantic chunk of cake was about four inches wide, six inches high, and nine inches long, and it looked as good as it was big.

After that, sated and pleasantly lethargic, we ambled through the rest of the museum, and to my delight, after days of searching antique shops for a soap dish in the exact right color, size and shape, I finally found exactly what I wanted locked inside a glass cage in the Asian section. The information plaque said it was from an ancient Chinese dynasty. I asked Doug if he believed the museum would sell it to me for four dollars.

He assumed the thoughtful air of a world-renowned glassware expert and studied it for a half minute before advising: "No. You'll have to come up to at least twenty."

Upon emerging from that satisfying foray into culture, we once again made the mistake of trusting the sloth who had authored our inadequate guidebook when we chose to use our remaining two hours of daylight to visit the Carillon Park in downtown Dayton, which, according to our guidebook, was a tiny, insignificant place, worthy of no more than a 10-minute glance. That casual dismissal of Carillon Park failed utterly to describe its size, depth, and full reality, and not knowing the truth denied us the ability to correctly apportion the amount of time needed to explore Carillon Park, for this sizable museum contained extensive exhibits dedicated to the many intriguing handiworks of the Wright Brothers who invented the airplane. We arrived an hour before the park closed and bought our tickets, not knowing we could never see more than a small portion of this museum in the one hour we had allocated for it.

The female clerk took our money, and without bothering to warn us how huge the museum was, said only in the weary, monotonous voice of someone ready to quit for the day and go home: "I'll start the Wright Robots."

We nodded indulgently, having no idea what she was referring to. Then she pulled a switch and we jumped back in alarm when two statues near us unexpectedly sprang to life and started "speaking" about themselves and their lives and inventions. They were Wilbur and Orville Wright as "animatronics"—the kind of thing you see in Disney World. After recovering from being so startled, Doug and I got the giggles watching them, yet even as we chuckled uncontrollably, something nagged me terribly. I did not voice my confusion, but physically they looked exactly like somebody I had seen somewhere in my past, though I couldn't put my finger on who it was.

Doug suddenly burst out with the answer: "It's Tom and Dick Smothers! Dickie's on the left, Tommy's on the right!!!"

The Wright Robots were dead ringers for the Smothers Brothers, the famous comedy team from the 1960s. Even their patter was hilariously similar to the "sibling competition" stage routines of the Smothers Brothers—"I designed it, Orville." "But I flew first, Wilbur." "But I flew the farthest, Orville." We were choking back our laughter, but if Wilbur/Tommy had said, "Mom always liked you best, Orville," we would have bellowed outright and collapsed into a thrashing fit on the floor. Had I been the programmer, I would have sneaked that in.

We barely heard anything the Wright Robots said; their similarity to Tommy and Dickie was too funny. With only 40 minutes left before the place closed, we raced through a few exhibits, getting the impression of two brothers who invented just for the love of their creative work. The photographs of them, made during their lifetimes, did not exhibit the extreme physical resemblance to the Smothers Brothers that the Wright Robots implied, a suspicious indicator that their programmers had deliberately modeled them after the comedy team just for laughs.

The park closed on us at five p.m., but we were slowing down anyhow and waddling a bit from our hugely satisfying museum lunch. In my inability to stop placing naïve trust in our misleading guidebook, I then chose the Miamisburg Mound as our final stop for the day, reasoning that a small, pleasant outdoor park would soothe our minds and bodies and whisk away the lingering effects of the crowds and recycled air that we had endured within the two indoor museums.

The Miamisburg Mound promotes itself as being the highest Indian Mound in Ohio, a believable claim, because the Miamisburg Mound was tall enough to block all views of the surrounding landscape and big enough to occupy most of the space in its small green park. The guidebook promised that after we climbed a long flight of stairs to the top of a viewing platform, we would be rewarded with an unsurpassed view of the Miami River and its related valley area.

We were the only people present, except for one man who was descending the stairs as we were ascending. He enthusiastically greeted us in a tone of starry-eyed awe as he swept by: "It's a great, great view!!"

We, even more eager now to see the great view that would confirm his five-star endorsement and bring our tiring day to a peaceful, perfect end, continued to the top and emerged onto a small viewing platform, about five feet square, to confront, directly in front of us and towering behind the Mound, a gigantic manufacturing plant, sporting a tangled array of towers and railings and smokestack-styled appendages, spewing clouds of unclassifiable gases and chemicals into the air. It was the only thing to be seen on that entire half of the viewing area.

Doug didn't miss a beat. In a magnificent tribute to brevity, he said: "That guy must be an engineer."

I was so overcome by the majesty of this great, great view that I slid slowly down onto the top step of that platform where I could safely sit and laugh as hard as I laughed without any danger of falling off when I lost control and toppled sideways. Doug dropped beside me, and we rested there, laughing and gazing into the small park beside the Mound, just a tiny section of trees and grass, containing no spectacular view, no river or valley—but also no steaming, smoking, choking manufacturing plant.

Back at the hotel, several children were knocking each other around in the parking lot and many more of them were clogging the lobby and the hallway to our room. I decided to relax and read while Doug left for the pool. Ten minutes later he returned, breathing hard and rapidly shutting and locking the door behind him, to advise me that his life was in danger from an army of kids between the ages of about 10 and 14. These kids were not only swarming the parking lot, the lobby and the hallways, but also about 200 of them were in the recreation area, which our room overlooked, throwing everything that would fit inside their chubby little hands into and across the pool, including tennis balls, ping-pong balls, and golf balls they had stolen from the putting area, either not realizing or not caring that severe injury can result from being hit with a golf ball.

Doug dropped onto the bed while saying in a disbelieving tone: "The hotel must have offered a deal. Bring one kid, get eight in for free, and the group that makes the most noise gets an all-night session lobbing balls into the pool."

Not a single supervising adult was visible anywhere, and all the security personnel who had provided such commanding comfort the night before had also disappeared, evidently holed up in some locked room and waiting out the siege until this group moved on.

We wanted a light meal, and the hotel map claimed the pool area contained a small café that would sell us something appropriate, but we couldn't find it. So Doug, after discreetly checking through our balcony doors to see how high those kids could hurl golf balls, stepped out on the balcony to determine if he could locate the cafe by sight from our high vantage point. He dodged back in to report: "The cafe is missing because those kids are playing soccer in it."

About 20 kids had set up a soccer game in the space belonging to the café, whose staff, facing this invasion, had abandoned their posts and hightailed it to safer territory.

Eventually we figured out that the town was hosting a soccer tournament, and the absence of parental guidance on public behaviour for that young mob was a consequence of the kids being there with chaperones, who, we were guessing, had gone to bed after downing two sleeping pills and a large mug of something alcoholic.

We escaped to a town restaurant for a late dinner, but wanting only a light meal, we ordered appetizers only, not realizing they were intended to be shared by six people. We ate half of our huge order, boxed up the remainder, and put it on ice in our cooler.

## Saturday, Day 9: Yellow Springs

**The Air Force Museum:** The next morning, when we checked out of the motel, the furious couple in front of us was demanding a full or at least a partial refund, citing the kids, the noise, and being unable to use the pool. We paid our bill without complaint and left, happy to escape. We skipped the hotel dining room, knowing it would be overrun with screaming kids, and tried a nearby family style restaurant for breakfast. Not a single parking space was available, and a disheveled string of kids lined the sidewalk from the door all the way out into the parking lot, all of them busily elbowing and kicking and scrapping with each other. To avoid eating where kids were winging biscuits past our heads and playing soccer with stacks of pancakes—and since all we wanted was coffee anyhow—Doug parked illegally and I kept a lookout while he ran inside to their takeout counter. He returned with two large coffees saying it was a good thing we were not hungry enough for breakfast as there was a 45-minute wait for a table.

Our first stop was the mammoth Air Force Museum, which, if you love the history and the mechanics of airplanes, is a great place to visit and you could spend weeks there. Otherwise, it doesn't take long to see it all because the planes blend together.

We had expected to spend an entire day, but we were barely into the first exhibit when I just wanted out. Although I spent five and a half years in the United States Air Force, and I am a big supporter of the military and of the necessity of a nation having a military, all I could see that day was the insanity of humanity. The exhibits were especially disorienting and dispiriting because they contrasted with the exuberant creativity of the Wright Brothers that we had experienced the day before, and that contrast emphasized how humanity had instantly transformed their marvelous contribution to human advancement into a weapon of war.

No matter which way I turned in that museum, I confronted the supremacy of human stupidity, which was matched only by the selfishness, self-importance, power hunger, and shortsightedness of the mid-20th century military leaders of America's Army and Navy in their reaction to the airplane. They resisted the formation of a fourth military branch, the Air Force, preferring to keep the planes under their own thumbs out of fear that an independent Air Force would reduce their personal power and importance. All I could think was, if you're going to use the invention of the airplane for war, then be logical and efficient about it, not petty and stupid. Only a total moron would not see that the airplane would become the superior weapon of war. If the goal of a military is national defense, then the political goals of all the military generals should be subverted to that. It was just plain stupid to let every other powerful nation create an air force equal to their armies and navies, while pretending, out of a petty need for personal importance, that our nation's Air Force should be kept small and insignificant, just an unimportant section of the Army—thus opening our country to being conquered. If the Allies hadn't had a strong air force during World War II, Germany would have won, for despite Hitler's many deficiencies, he was still smart enough to see how to use the airplane for conquering other nations.

I raced through the exhibits, taking time only for the ones on the Berlin Airlift and the Holocaust, which is such a horror that I never read about it or watch movies about it, but that day I decided that if humanity were going to use creative inventions for destruction, then by damn, people should stare straight into the face of that destruction. So, I stopped and looked, though neither exhibit lifted my mood, as both the Berlin Airlift and the Holocaust were nothing but gigantic wastes of human and material resources to exalt stupidity.

The Holocaust is well known to most people, but the nature of the Berlin Airlift is not so well known. According to the exhibit, the Berlin Airlift came about when the Soviet Union got ticked off about not being able to control the currency, so they blockaded the city out of petty spite. This necessitated a gigantic expenditure of resources—people, fuel, planes, supplies, man-hours—in flying supplies to the citizens, an expenditure that could have served a far better purpose had it not been so badly needed to counter their abject stupidity.

Before departing the Air Force Museum, we attempted to buy lunch at the museum's café, a place the size of a baseball field that was packed with a mass of shifting, gobbling, noisy people in search of food. After struggling to get within shouting distance of where the line appeared to begin, we abandoned even the idea of eating there, escaped to our vehicle in the parking lot, raided our cooler for fruit juice and leftover appetizers from our late dinner the previous night, and picnicked on the grass. It was not the best meal I've ever had, but it was filling and quiet.

**Yellow Springs:** Yellow Springs is one weird little town, just east of Dayton, that has never escaped the '60s, and entering it from a military museum was like sliding from one dimension into another. Little hippie shops lined the streets where old, ex-hippies were playing for donations, something I hadn't seen since London in 1973. At the B&B where we stayed, we parked in between a car that sported a Grateful Dead bumper sticker and one covered with signs encouraging us to "Save Tibet."

According to the brochure, the B&B, built in 1921, was the former home of an Antioch College president, after which it became a college dormitory, then an office, then a food co-op before being turned into a B&B. The clean interior was well maintained, but our only greeting was a card in the lobby with written instructions directing us to our room and, to Doug's profound gratitude, a full-size bed. No key was provided, and without a key, we left our bags locked in the truck while we explored the town.

Everything we wanted to see lay within walking distance, so we collected a brochure and a map of their historic district, which included construction dates for its houses and the reasons for their historic value, and started up the street past a guy seated at an outdoor café, wearing a T-shirt that said, "He's dead and I'm grateful." We stepped over and around people sprawled on sidewalks, passing smokes back and forth, and made our way to a dairy bar for soft drinks before sauntering on.

A couple in their early thirties, out in their yard and busily engaged with the not-so-easy task of restoring their ancient Victorian house, noticed us gawking at the houses and struck up a chat. They were jokingly annoyed that their house was not on our list as they were certain it was at least 50 to 75 years older than the 60 years the local historical society credited it with being, but they lacked documentation to prove it. Doug (an architect) checked the foundation and told them they were probably right about the house's true age. Apparently stone foundations were not often used after the 1920s, and theirs was stone.

At almost six p.m., we meandered back into the downtown area to eat at the one really good, sit-down restaurant in town, the Winds Café. We assumed the dinner crowd would not arrive for another hour, but we failed to consider that it was Saturday night. Their dining room and outdoor patio were stuffed with people who were out on the town to eat and generate as much noise as possible. The only available table was in the bar. When we hesitated, the hostess assured us we would get full service. A tiny, two-person table in a noisy bar, even one out in the open and well lit by sunlight flowing in through the glass doors leading to the patio, was not our preference, but neither was sitting on the curb outside the Dairy Freeze, balancing a bad hot dog and cold fries.

We took the table, but before we were served our excellent dinner, I visited the toilet to wash off the day's grunge. Ordinarily we shower and change before dinner, but we had been closed out of too many restaurants by taking the time to make ourselves presentable. We had arrived at the Winds the moment they opened for dinner, and we still almost failed to get a table.

After using the toilet, I was preparing to go wash my hands when I glanced into the bowl to ensure it had flushed properly and saw that it had refilled with a golden yellow liquid, similar to the color I had deposited to be flushed out. As I left the stall, a woman entered the restroom, and not wanting her to think I had left an unsanitary toilet, I said, "If you use this, I want you to know that I flushed it, but it refilled with this golden color."

She replied, "Oh hon, that's just Yellow Springs," and sailed into the stall.

**Sunday, Day 10: Home Again**

I did not sleep well in that B&B because I underwent a genuinely weird experience. I woke in the middle of the night to find myself in another time period, the early 1900s. Several other people were present in the room wearing clothes from that era. Although no key had been provided for our room, we could and did lock the door from the inside; thus no one had entered our room after we went to bed. For some reason I cannot explain, I did not want to know what was happening. I instantly closed out the people and the time period and returned to sleep. When I woke in the morning, the other people and the other time had vanished along with all details and reasons for the experience. For some reason I also cannot explain, I did not retain and question and ponder the incident the way I normally do such things. I did not just ignore it; I chose to utterly forget it. I simply shrugged and said dismissively, "Those things happen," and blanked it from my mind. But now, years later, I wonder why I reacted in such a way contrary to my nature.

We were first to the breakfast table at seven-thirty, and we were nearly finished when another couple joined us. He introduced her and got her name wrong, called her something that rhymed with her name, something like Terry when it was Carrie or Sherry. She let it pass, but the look she gave him promised doom for their apparently brand-new relationship.

We left for home on a beautiful morning, and just outside Yellow Springs, we gambled on a small detour to Clifton Gorge, a nature preserve that our guidebook dismissed as barely worth seeing. By this time, I knew that the only successful way to use our guidebook was to do and believe the opposite of whatever it said. A wise decision, for how the author could enthusiastically promote the first stop of our trip on our first day—a gravel pull-off to an overgrown and non-existent trail leading to a small cliff—and dismiss Clifton Gorge as nothing worth seeing was incomprehensible. Clifton Gorge was worth an entire day, but we had only an hour or two.

The gorge was a former dwelling place for the Shawnee Indians, who retreated to its substantially cooler bottom during summers to escape the heat. We descended into the gorge and hiked about a fourth of the trail, deducing as we went, that because all the hiking trails followed the easier descents and ascents, they had been built on top of the natural trails the Indians had used. The trails and the morning silence made it easy to imagine the presence of the Shawnees.

Our assumption that no one else would be there at such an early hour, about eight-thirty, enabled a female runner and a male hiker to surprise us with their company. The male hiker appeared fortuitously as we were studying a trail map and trying to decide whether to return to the top from where we were or take a chance that other trails to the top would appear. He lived in the area, knew the trails well, and warned us that the only trails to the top were the ones at the far ends and the one we were standing at. We had not brought adequate water to hike the entire trail, and we lacked the time anyhow. So we walked only a small bit farther to the Blue Pool, then turned around and retraced our steps.

A few miles up the road from Clifton Gorge, we stopped at the Clifton Mill—a mill restored to capitalize on the nostalgia craze, where, quite unexpectedly for a Sunday morning, the place was jammed with people, all of whom were greedily swarming the gift shop as if at a 90-percent-off clearance sale. As the only two visitors who were curious as to how the mill operated—and had no compulsive yearning to fill a shopping bag with useless knickknacks—we elbowed our way through the packed crowd to reach a young man who was working his way through college by running the mill. He gave us a private tour, and at the end, in an energetic spurt of gratitude for our curiosity, he proudly presented us with a small sample bag of the product of his labor.

As we departed the mill, I plucked a brochure off a rack advertising a B&B in the nearby small town of South Charleston, and we started home to Columbus in a state of hearty cheer that our little 10-day drive in the country had been, overall, the enjoyable and restful trip we had desired. It was, we agreed, not just the best vacation we had ever taken, but the only one we had ever taken that could be defined as a true vacation from demands and deadlines. Doug felt so expansive that when we reached South

Charleston, he agreed to swing past the B&B to take a look at a quite nice, old and restored Victorian house.

I was reading the brochure information out loud, which boasted that one of their rooms offered a "three-quarter antique bed," but that bit of helpful information had barely exited my mouth when Doug, still nurturing the painful crick in his neck from our first night in a B&B, said instantly: "No way. I've been there. And the quarter that was missing was where my head was supposed to go."

# Conclusion

Laughter keeps us mentally, emotionally, and physically healthy.

During my twenties, a coworker commented on my habit of humming to myself while I worked by asking, "Why are you always so happy?"

I replied, "Because I have two choices in life. I can be happy or I can be unhappy. I have chosen to be happy."

She said in a know-it-all tone that combined contempt and condescension, "Well, you can say that if you've never had any problems."

I said nothing, but I thought, *Oh, if you only knew.*

I take a special, private pride in knowing that not one person who has ever met me has ever suspected (and the truth would have shocked them) the nightmare that was the first 22 years of my life, a nightmare so bad that it nearly destroyed me mentally, emotionally, and physically—but it didn't, because, when I was only 17, I began laughing at the lunacies of living.

www.ingramcontent.com/pod-product-compliance
Lightning Source LLC
Chambersburg PA
CBHW060018100426
42740CB00010B/1519